PRE-ALGEBRA

Author: Myrl Shireman

Editor: Mary Dieterich

Proofreaders: April Albert and Margaret Brown

COPYRIGHT © 2018 Mark Twain Media, Inc.

ISBN 978-1-62223-702-9

Printing No. CD-405025

Mark Twain Media, Inc., Publishers
Distributed by Carson-Dellosa Publishing LLC

Table of Contents

Table of Contents *(continued)*

Introduction

A challenge facing U.S. educators is that of increasing the number of high school students completing mathematics course work to the algebra level and beyond. This has become a critical issue since many of today's high school graduates do not possess the mathematics skills necessary for the modern workplace.

Many students find the concepts presented in algebra to be abstract, and they become discouraged. In far too many cases, students have not had sufficient opportunity to practice those algebra concepts, which appear more abstract than they really are.

This book is designed to help students become familiar with some of the basic concepts necessary for success in algebra. The concepts chosen are those that must be understood to succeed in problem-solving activities, which are a vital part of high school mathematics.

Teachers are encouraged to make copies and transparencies of this book to use in guided and independent practice. The pages can also be scanned to make digital files, and the e-book version is already in a digital format that can be used with the teacher providing guidance as the activities are completed on a classroom Whiteboard, a computer projection device, or on individual computers. Guided practice to assure understanding is the key to successfully completing independent practice and developing a positive attitude toward algebra.

—THE AUTHOR

Name: _____ Date: _____

Number Systems

The number systems you are most familiar with are the counting numbers and the whole numbers. The **counting numbers** begin with the number 1, while the whole numbers begin with 0. So **whole numbers**, which you have used often, include the counting numbers plus 0.

In your study of algebra, you will need to get to know another number system to solve problems. These new numbers are called the integer numbers. The **integer numbers** include the whole numbers and a new set of numbers known as negative numbers. The integers are called signed numbers since they include both positive and negative numbers.

Let's review the number systems we have talked about.

1, 2, 3, 4, 5, 6, 7, 8, 9 . . . Counting Numbers

0, 1, 2, 3, 4, 5, 6, 7, 8, 9 . . . Whole Numbers

. . . -9, -8, -7, -6, -5, -4, -3, -2, -1, 0, +1, +2, +3, +4, +5, +6, +7, +8, +9 . . . Integer Numbers

The integers include numbers to the right and left of 0. The numbers on the right are **positive** and are noted with the small plus (+) sign. Positive numbers may also be written without the plus sign. The numbers on the left side of 0 are the **negative numbers**, and they are noted with the small minus (-) sign. Remember, the integers are known as signed numbers.

. . . -8 -7 -6 -5 -4 -3 -2 -1 0 +1 +2 +3 +4 +5 +6 +7 +8 . . .

$\longleftarrow$ _____ _____ $\longrightarrow$

You can see on the above number line that the integers to the right and left of 0 are exactly the same *except* for the sign. Any given number on the right has an opposite number on the left. The +5 integer has an opposite on the left, and it is -5. All numbers except 0 also have an opposite.

Directions: Fill in the following blanks with words from the reading that complete each sentence.

Counting numbers begin with the number **1.** _____. Whole numbers begin with **2.** _____. Whole numbers include the counting numbers plus **3.** _____. The integer number system includes positive and **4.** _____ numbers. Those integers to the left of 0 have a **5.** _____ sign, while those to the right have a **6.** _____ sign.

Integer numbers have opposites. The opposite of +4 is **7.** _____. The opposite of -7 is **8.** _____. The opposite of +60 is **9.** _____.

Name: _____ Date: _____

The Integer Number System

A number line can be helpful in understanding the **integer number system**—a number system that you use quite frequently in your daily life.

Let's use the number line below to keep track of the yards lost and gained in a football game. The distance between each number represents 1 yard. Let's say your team has a first down and gains 7 yards. This is a gain, so it is represented on the number line by +7. Now on the second down, your team loses 4 yards. A four-yard loss is a -4, so this is represented by showing a -4-yard move to the left from +7. So for the two downs, your team has a net gain of +3 yards.

1st down gain →

← 2nd down loss

. . . -10 -9 -8 -7 -6 -5 -4 -3 -2 -1 0 +1 +2 +3 +4 +5 +6 +7 +8 +9 +10 . . .

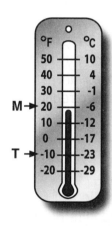

A thermometer, which is much like a number line, can be used to understand positive and negative numbers. Let's say you live where the winters are very cold. Monday you leave for school and the temperature is 20°F. Since the 20 is a positive number, it is 20° above 0, which has been marked with the letter "M" for Monday. Now on Tuesday, you leave for school and note the mercury in the thermometer is at point "T" for Tuesday. Since the "T" is by the 10 below 0, it has a negative sign, and you say it is 10° below zero.

Let's practice with the number line below so that you become comfortable with using positive and negative numbers. Point A is at +5 on the number line. If you were told to move +3 places, you would move 3 places to the right of "A" and be at Point "B" or at +8. If you were told to move -3 places from Point A, you would be at Point C, which is located at +2.

C ___-3___ A ___+3___ B

. . . -10 -9 -8 -7 -6 -5 -4 -3 -2 -1 0 +1 +2 +3 +4 +5 +6 +7 +8 +9 +10 . . .

Name: _____ Date: _____

The Integer Number System (continued)

Directions: Use the number line below to locate the following.

1. +3 places from +10 is at _____

2. -4 places from +6 is at _____

3. +8 places from -9 is at _____

4. -7 places from +3 is at _____

5. +10 places from -4 is at _____

6. -4 places from -2 is at _____

7. -6 places from -6 is at _____

. . . -13 -12 -11 -10 -9 -8 -7 -6 -5 -4 -3 -2 -1 0 +1 +2 +3 +4 +5 +6 +7 +8 +9 +10 +11 +12 +13 . . .

Directions: Use the number line above to answer the questions that follow.

8. To get from +4 to +9 you must move _____ spaces in the positive direction.

9. To get from -3 to -9 you must move _____ spaces in the _____ direction.

10. To get from +3 to -4 you must move _____ spaces in the _____ direction.

11. To get from -2 to +6 you must move _____ spaces in the _____ direction.

Review: Integers on a number line

Those integers on a number line to the left of zero are called **12.** _____ numbers. The integers to the right of zero are called **13.** _____ numbers. Integers have opposites. The opposite of -7 is +7. What is the opposite of each of the following?

14. +2 is opposite _____

15. -40 is opposite _____

16. +800 is opposite _____

17. +6 is opposite _____

18. -249 is opposite _____

19. +2,101 is opposite _____

20. -5,732 is opposite _____

Name: _____ Date: _____

Number Properties

In algebra, you will study number properties. These properties are known as **commutative**, **associative**, and **distributive**.

The *commutative property of addition* says that the order in which you add whole numbers will not change the sum. For example, 5 + 3 = 8 and 3 + 5 = 8, so 5 + 3 = 3 + 5.

In your study of algebra, you will often see letters used to stand in for numbers. These letters are called **unknowns**. You will see the commutative property for addition stated as $a + b = b + a$ where a and b are unknown and can be any whole numbers.

Directions: Complete the following.

Solve so that
$a + b = b + a$

1. 7 + 3 = _____ so _____ + 7 = 10

2. 25 + _____ = 35 so 10 + _____ = 35

3. 210 + 150 = _____ so 150 + _____ = 360

4. 84 + _____ = 104 so _____ + 84 = 104

5. 25 + _____ = 90 so 65 + _____ = 90

Directions: Complete the following using $a + b = b + a$ when you fill in the blank for each problem.

$$a + b = b + a$$

6. 5 + 7 = 7 + 5 $a = 5$ $b = 7$

7. _____ + _____ = _____ + _____ $a = 35$ $b = 64$

8. _____ + _____ = _____ + _____ $a = 111$ $b = 742$

9. _____ + _____ = _____ + _____ $a = 37$ $b = 94$

10. _____ + _____ = _____ + _____ $a = 2,101$ $b = 642$

11. _____ + _____ = _____ + _____ $a = 10$ $b = 18$

12. _____ + _____ = _____ + _____ $a = 12$ $b = 23$

Name: _____   Date: _____

Whole Numbers

Using the number line below, place a dot to represent the answer for each problem. The number line represents part of the whole number system.

Example: 3 + 1 + 2 = 6, so a dot is placed below 6 on the number line.

0 1 2 3 4 5 6 7 8 9 10 11 12 13 14 15 16 17 18 19
$\longrightarrow$
•

Directions: Solve the following. Then place a dot on the number line beneath the correct answer for each problem.

1. 7 + 3 + 1 = _____

2. 1 + 7 + 3 = _____

3. 5 + 4 + 2 = _____

4. 2 + 4 + 5 = _____

5. 3 + 6 + 4 = _____

6. 4 + 3 + 6 = _____

7. 8 + 2 + 1 = _____

8. 2 + 1 + 8 = _____

9. 2 + 4 + 3 + 5 = _____

10. 3 + 5 + 2 + 4 = _____

11. The order in which whole numbers are added does not change the _____.

Another important thing to remember is that when whole numbers are added, the sum is *always* another whole number. A special term is applied to this fact. The special term is ***closure***. It means that the whole number system is closed for addition; therefore, when whole numbers are added, the sum is another whole number.

Name: _____ Date: _____

Commutative Property for Multiplication

The *commutative property for multiplication* states that the order in which whole numbers are multiplied does not change the product. For example, $3 \cdot 7 = 7 \cdot 3$. In algebra you will see this stated as $a \cdot b = b \cdot a$ when any whole numbers can replace the unknowns a and b.

Directions: Solve the following.

1. $4 \cdot 3 =$ _____ **2.** $3 \cdot 4 =$ _____ **3.** $2 \cdot 5 =$ _____ **4.** $5 \cdot 2 =$ _____

5. $3 \cdot 7 =$ _____ **6.** $7 \cdot 3 =$ _____ **7.** $10 \cdot 2 =$ _____ **8.** $2 \cdot 10 =$ _____

Notice in the above problems that the order of multiplying the numbers does not change the product. Also, you will see that all of the products are whole numbers. When whole numbers are multiplied, the product is another whole number. So multiplication is closed for the multiplication of whole numbers. Remember, the special term applied for this fact is **closure**.

Directions: Complete the following using the numbers given for a and b for each problem.

Example: $2 \cdot 7 = 7 \cdot 2$ $a = 2$ $b = 7$

9. _____ $\cdot$ _____ $=$ _____ $\cdot$ _____ $a = 5$ $b = 4$

10. _____ $\cdot$ _____ $=$ _____ $\cdot$ _____ $a = 12$ $b = 6$

11. _____ $\cdot$ _____ $=$ _____ $\cdot$ _____ $a = 111$ $b = 246$

12. _____ $\cdot$ _____ $=$ _____ $\cdot$ _____ $a = 1,074$ $b = 917$

13. _____ $\cdot$ _____ $=$ _____ $\cdot$ _____ $a = 47$ $b = 86$

The fact that you can change the order of whole numbers when multiplying can be helpful. Solve the following.

14. $\begin{array}{r} 40 \\ \times\ 86 \\ \hline \end{array}$ **15.** $\begin{array}{r} 86 \\ \times\ 40 \\ \hline \end{array}$ **16.** $\begin{array}{r} 800 \\ \times\ 770 \\ \hline \end{array}$ **17.** $\begin{array}{r} 770 \\ \times\ 800 \\ \hline \end{array}$

Did you get the same answer for problems 14 and 15 and the same answer for problems 16 and 17?

18. Which problem was easier to solve, 14 or 15? _____

19. Which problem was easier to solve, 16 or 17? _____

20. Can you explain why it was easier to solve two of the problems? _____

_____

Name: _____ Date: _____

Associative Property for Addition

Directions: In the following problems, add the numbers in the parentheses first, and then add the number outside the parentheses.

add first

Example: $6 + (3 + 4) = 6 + 7 = 13$

1. $8 + (5 + 2) =$ _____ + _____ = _____

7. $(12 + 3) + 5 =$ _____ + _____ = _____

2. $(8 + 5) + 2 =$ _____ + _____ = _____

8. $12 + (3 + 5) =$ _____ + _____ = _____

3. $(8 + 2) + 5 =$ _____ + _____ = _____

9. $(12 + 5) + 3 =$ _____ + _____ = _____

4. $9 + (6 + 1) =$ _____ + _____ = _____

10. $10 + (6 + 7) =$ _____ + _____ = _____

5. $(9 + 6) + 1 =$ _____ + _____ = _____

11. $(10 + 6) + 7 =$ _____ + _____ = _____

6. $(9 + 1) + 6 =$ _____ + _____ = _____

12. $(7 + 10) + 6 =$ _____ + _____ = _____

From the work above, you can see that the order in which you add the numbers in a problem does not change the answer. This property of addition is called the *associative property for addition.* You can use this property to help make it easier to solve addition problems.

Directions: Solve the following (rearrange the numbers to make the problems as easy as you can).

13. $9 + 8 + 4 + 1 = ($ _____ + _____ $) + ($ _____ + _____ $) =$ _____

14. $1 + 12 + 8 + 4 = ($ _____ + _____ $) + ($ _____ + _____ $) =$ _____

15. $14 + 3 + 6 + 9 = ($ _____ + _____ $) + ($ _____ + _____ $) =$ _____

16. $18 + 7 + 10 + 7 = ($ _____ + _____ $) + ($ _____ + _____ $) =$ _____

17. $25 + 16 + 5 + 4 = ($ _____ + _____ $) + ($ _____ + _____ $) =$ _____

18. $29 + 4 + 16 + 10 = ($ _____ + _____ $) + ($ _____ + _____ $) =$ _____

19. $61 + 14 + 6 + 9 = ($ _____ + _____ $) + ($ _____ + _____ $) =$ _____

20. $13 + 6 + 7 + 11 = ($ _____ + _____ $) + ($ _____ + _____ $) =$ _____

Name: _____ Date: _____

Associative Property for Multiplication

Directions: In the problems below, multiply the numbers between the parentheses first. Then multiply that answer by the number outside the parentheses.

multiply first
↓
Example: $(7 \cdot 5) \cdot 3 = 35 \cdot 3 = 105$

1. $(6 \cdot 3) \cdot 4 =$ _____ $\cdot$ _____ $=$ _____

2. $6 \cdot (3 \cdot 4) =$ _____ $\cdot$ _____ $=$ _____

3. $3 \cdot (6 \cdot 4) =$ _____ $\cdot$ _____ $=$ _____

4. $(9 \cdot 4) \cdot 5 =$ _____ $\cdot$ _____ $=$ _____

5. $9 \cdot (4 \cdot 5) =$ _____ $\cdot$ _____ $=$ _____

6. $(9 \cdot 5) \cdot 4 =$ _____ $\cdot$ _____ $=$ _____

7. $(12 \cdot 2) \cdot 6 =$ _____ $\cdot$ _____ $=$ _____

8. $12 \cdot (2 \cdot 6) =$ _____ $\cdot$ _____ $=$ _____

9. $(6 \cdot 12) \cdot 2 =$ _____ $\cdot$ _____ $=$ _____

10. $(15 \cdot 3) \cdot 5 =$ _____ $\cdot$ _____ $=$ _____

11. $15 \cdot (3 \cdot 5) =$ _____ $\cdot$ _____ $=$ _____

12. $3 \cdot (15 \cdot 5) =$ _____ $\cdot$ _____ $=$ _____

In multiplying the above problems, the order in which the numbers are multiplied does not change the product. This is known as the *associative property for multiplication.* You will find that this property allows you to rearrange numbers and can make problems easier to solve.

Directions: Solve the following (rearrange the numbers to make the problems as easy as possible).

Example: $6 \cdot 3 \cdot 5 \cdot 2 = (6 \cdot 5) \cdot (3 \cdot 2) = 30 \cdot 6 = 180$

13. $15 \cdot 3 \cdot 6 \cdot 5 = ($ _____ $\cdot$ _____ $) \cdot ($ _____ $\cdot$ _____ $) = ($ _____ $) \cdot ($ _____ $) =$ _____

14. $5 \cdot 12 \cdot 2 \cdot 8 = ($ _____ $\cdot$ _____ $) \cdot ($ _____ $\cdot$ _____ $) = ($ _____ $) \cdot ($ _____ $) =$ _____

15. $8 \cdot 3 \cdot 5 \cdot 2 = ($ _____ $\cdot$ _____ $) \cdot ($ _____ $\cdot$ _____ $) = ($ _____ $) \cdot ($ _____ $) =$ _____

16. $14 \cdot 8 \cdot 5 \cdot 4 = ($ _____ $\cdot$ _____ $) \cdot ($ _____ $\cdot$ _____ $) = ($ _____ $) \cdot ($ _____ $) =$ _____

17. $17 \cdot 2 \cdot 8 \cdot 5 = ($ _____ $\cdot$ _____ $) \cdot ($ _____ $\cdot$ _____ $) = ($ _____ $) \cdot ($ _____ $) =$ _____

18. $3 \cdot 5 \cdot 24 \cdot 2 = ($ _____ $\cdot$ _____ $) \cdot ($ _____ $\cdot$ _____ $) = ($ _____ $) \cdot ($ _____ $) =$ _____

19. $25 \cdot 5 \cdot 2 \cdot 4 = ($ _____ $\cdot$ _____ $) \cdot ($ _____ $\cdot$ _____ $) = ($ _____ $) \cdot ($ _____ $) =$ _____

20. $3 \cdot 10 \cdot 6 \cdot 11 = ($ _____ $\cdot$ _____ $) \cdot ($ _____ $\cdot$ _____ $) = ($ _____ $) \cdot ($ _____ $) =$ _____

Name: _____ Date: _____

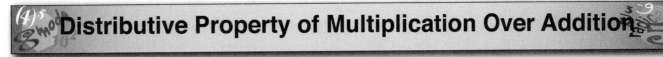

Distributive Property of Multiplication Over Addition

Another very important number property that can be used with whole numbers is the *distributive property of multiplication over addition*. This property lets you take a problem like 5 • 46 and rewrite it as follows. First, write it as 5 • (40 + 6). Then you can go a step farther to simplify the problem and rewrite it again as (5 • 40) + (5 • 6). This rewriting often makes it easier to solve the problem.

Directions: Solve the following.

Example: 8 • 46 = 8 • (40 + 6) = (8 • 40) + (8 • 6) = 320 + 48 = 368

1. 5 • 36 = 5 • (_____ + _____) = (5 • 30) + (5 • _____) = _____ + _____ = _____

2. 9 • 42 = 9 • (_____ + _____) = (9 • _____) + (9 • _____) = _____ + _____ = _____

3. 12 • 88 = 12 • (_____ + _____) = (12 • _____) + (12 • _____) = _____ + _____ = _____

4. 7 • 35 = 7 • (_____ + _____) = (7 • _____) + (7 • _____) = _____ + _____ = _____

5. 6 • 78 = 6 • (_____ + _____) = (6 • _____) + (6 • _____) = _____ + _____ = _____

6. 8 • 48 = 8 • (_____ + _____) = (8 • _____) + (8 • _____) = _____ + _____ = _____

7. 14 • 268 = 14 • (_____ + _____) = (14 • _____) + (14 • _____) = _____ + _____ = _____

8. 18 • 160 = 18 • (_____ + _____) = (18 • _____) + (18 • _____) = _____ + _____ = _____

9. 3 • 38 = 3 • (_____ + _____) = (3 • _____) + (3 • _____) = _____ + _____ = _____

10. 11 • 79 = 11 • (_____ + _____) = (11 • _____) + (11 • _____) = _____ + _____ = _____

Properties of Subtraction and Division

Do the same number properties work with subtraction and division? The commutative properties for multiplication and addition let you multiply or add whole numbers in any order and get the correct product or sum. Will the commutative property work for subtraction? Does $a - b = b - a$? If $a = 4$ and $b = 2$, does $4 - 2 = 2 - 4$? No, because $4 - 2 = 2$, while $2 - 4 = -2$. So $a - b$ does **not** equal $b - a$. You will note that -2 is not a whole number; it is a negative number and part of the integer number system.

What about the commutative property and division? Does $a \div b = b \div a$? If $a = 4$ and $b = 2$, does $4 \div 2 = 2 \div 4$? No, because $4 \div 2 = 2$, while $2 \div 4 = \frac{1}{2}$. So $a \div b$ does not equal $b \div a$.

The commutative property does not work for subtraction or division problems.

Will the associative property work for subtraction? Will $(a - b) - c = a - (b - c)$? If $a = 8$, $b = 4$, and $c = 2$, then $(8 - 4) - 2 = 2$, but $8 - (4 - 2) = 6$. $(a - b) - c$ does not equal $a - (b - c)$.

Does the associative property work for division? Does $(a \div b) \div c = a \div (b \div c)$? If $a = 8$, $b = 4$, and $c = 2$, then $(8 \div 4) \div 2 = 1$, but $8 \div (4 \div 2) = 4$. So $(a \div b) \div c$ does not equal $a \div (b \div c)$.

The associative property does not work for subtraction or division.

Directions: For the next exercise you will use two symbols. The symbols are (=) for equals and (≠) for does not equal. Insert the correct symbol (= or ≠) in the blank in each of the following problems.

Example: $a \cdot b = b \cdot a$
($a \cdot b$ equals $b \cdot a$, so the symbol = goes in the blank)

> Remember to check each problem to determine if = or ≠ is correct. Substitute $a = 8$, $b = 4$, and $c = 2$, and work each problem.

1. $a + b$ _____ $b + a$

2. $a \cdot (b \cdot c)$ _____ $(a \cdot b) \cdot c$

3. $a + (b + c)$ _____ $(a + b) + c$

4. $a - b$ _____ $b - a$

5. $a \div b$ _____ $b \div a$

6. $a - (b - c)$ _____ $(a - b) - c$

7. $a \div (b \div c)$ _____ $(a \div b) \div c$

Name: _____   Date: _____

Properties of Zero/Identity Elements

Zero is a special number in our numeration system. Zero never has a positive or negative sign associated with it. So when zero is added to any number, the answer is always the number to which zero is added. This is known as the *identity element for addition.*

$$5 + 0 = 5 \qquad\qquad 12 + 0 = 12 \qquad\qquad 180 + 0 = 180$$
$$0 + 5 = 5 \qquad\qquad 0 + 12 = 12 \qquad\qquad 0 + 180 = 180$$

In algebra you will see the identity element for addition stated as $a + 0 = a$ and $0 + a = a$.

Zero has another property called the *multiplication property of zero*. This property states that if zero is multiplied by any number, the result is always zero.

$$5 \cdot 0 = 0 \qquad\qquad 0 \cdot 114 = 0 \qquad\qquad 28 \cdot 0 = 0$$
$$0 \cdot 9 = 0 \qquad\qquad 12 \cdot 0 = 0 \qquad\qquad 0 \cdot 13 = 0$$

In algebra this property is often stated as $a \cdot 0 = 0$ and $0 \cdot a = 0$.

The *identity element for multiplication* says that when any number is multiplied by 1, the answer will always be the number being multiplied by one. In algebra books you will often see the identity element for multiplication stated as $a \cdot 1 = a$ and $1 \cdot a = a$.

Answer the following.

1. When zero is added to any number, the answer is always the _____ to which zero has been added.

2. When zero is multiplied by any number, the answer is always _____.

3. The identity element for multiplication says that when any number is multiplied by _____, the answer will always be the number being multiplied by 1.

Directions: Place the letter that matches the definition of the property demonstrated in each problem in the space before it. The first one is done for you.

A. Identity element for addition   B. Identity element for multiplication
C. Multiplication property of zero

4. __A__ $8 + 0 = 8$ **7.** _____ $0 + 48 = 48$ **10.** _____ $96 \cdot 1 = 96$

5. _____ $9 \cdot 1 = 9$ **8.** _____ $1 \cdot 17 = 17$ **11.** _____ $1 \cdot 124 = 124$

6. _____ $4 \cdot 0 = 0$ **9.** _____ $17 \cdot 1 = 17$ **12.** _____ $47 \cdot 0 = 0$

Name: _____ Date: _____

Order of Operations

In many problems you will find that you must perform more than one operation. There is an order in which you should perform the operations to get the correct answer. The order is to <u>multiply or divide</u> first from left to right, and then <u>subtract or add</u> from left to right.

Example: In the problem $8 \cdot 7 + 5 \cdot 4$, the multiplication will be performed first and then the addition. So $8 \cdot 7 + 5 \cdot 4$ becomes $56 + 20 = 76$

Directions: Solve the following (multiply first).

1. $5 \cdot 4 + 3 \cdot 2 =$ _____ + _____ = _____   **3.** $4 \cdot 8 + 7 \cdot 2 =$ _____ + _____ = _____

2. $6 \cdot 9 + 3 \cdot 8 =$ _____ + _____ = _____   **4.** $2 \cdot 9 + 4 \cdot 3 =$ _____ + _____ = _____

Directions: Solve the following (multiply first).

5. $5 \cdot 4 - 3 \cdot 2 =$ _____ − _____ = _____   **7.** $4 \cdot 8 - 7 \cdot 2 =$ _____ − _____ = _____

6. $6 \cdot 9 - 3 \cdot 8 =$ _____ − _____ = _____   **8.** $2 \cdot 9 - 4 \cdot 3 =$ _____ − _____ = _____

When a problem includes multiplication, division, addition, and subtraction, perform the multiplication or division first from left to right and then the addition or subtraction from left to right.

Example: $4 \cdot 7 - 3 \cdot 4 \div 2 = 28 - 12 \div 2 = 28 - 6 = 22$

Directions: Solve the following (follow the order of operations).

9. $3 \cdot 8 + 8 \div 2 =$ _____ $+ 8 \div 2 =$ _____ + _____ = _____

10. $14 \div 7 + 4 \cdot 8 - 6 =$ _____ $+ 4 \cdot 8 - 6 =$ _____ + _____ − 6 = _____ − 6 = _____

11. $7 + 3 \cdot 8 - 8 \div 2 = 7 +$ _____ $- 8 \div 2 = 7 +$ _____ − _____ = _____ − _____ = _____

12. $6 \cdot 5 - 16 \div 8 + 4 =$ _____ $- 16 \div 8 + 4 =$ _____ − _____ + 4 = _____ + 4 = _____

13. $5 \cdot 4 + 28 \div 7 - 4 =$ _____ $+ 28 \div 7 - 4 =$ _____ + _____ − 4 = _____ − 4 = _____

Name: _____ Date: _____

Addition of Integers

A number line can be helpful when learning to add integers.

. . . -14 -13 -12 -11 -10 -9 -8 -7 -6 -5 -4 -3 -2 -1 0 +1 +2 +3 +4 +5 +6 +7 +8 +9 +10 +11 +12 +13 +14 . . .

Follow the directions and solve this problem. On the number line above, draw a dot over the -7. Since you are adding a +9, now draw an arrow beginning at -7 and move +9 places to the right. If you move +9 places right from -7, the tip of the arrow will be over +2. So if you add -7 + +9 you get +2.

```
Add    -7
    +  +9
```

Directions: Solve these addition problems. Use the number line if you need to. Remember to start at zero.

| | | | | | | | | | | | | | 0 | | | | | | | | | | | | |

1.
```
    +5
+  +6
```

2.
```
    -5
+  -3
```

3.
```
   -10
+   +6
```

4.
```
    +9
+  -6
```

5.
```
    -8
+  +2
```

6.
```
    -3
+  -7
```

7.
```
    +6
+  +2
```

8.
```
    +7
+   0
```

Let's make some rules for adding positive and negative integers:

Rule 1: When adding two integers with the same sign, add the numbers and place the sign of the numbers before the answer.

Example:

```
Add    +5
    +  +6
       +11
```
When adding (+5) + (+6) = +11, both 5 and 6 have a positive sign, so the answer also has a positive sign.

Rule 2: *When adding two numbers with unlike signs, first find the difference between the two numbers. Then place the sign of the larger number before the answer.*

Example A:

```
Add    +8
    +  -2
       +6
```
Think 8 – 2 = 6. The larger number is +8, so the sign before the answer is positive.

Example B:

```
Add    -12
    +  +4
       -8
```
Think 12 – 4 = 8. The sign before the larger number is minus, so the sign before the answer is minus.

Name: _____ Date: _____

Addition of Integers: Exercises

Directions: Write the rules for adding two integers in the space below.

Rule 1: _____

_____

_____

Rule 2: _____

_____

_____

Directions: Add (refer to your rules if needed).

1.   +6
+ +4

2.   -4
+ -3

3.   +10
+   -4

4.   -8
+ +3

5.   +12
+   -9

6.   -372
+ +111

7.   +84
+ -16

8. +406
+ -305

9.   -67
+ +52

10.   -44
+ -21

11.   -16
+ +14

12. +31
+ -14

13. +146
+   -32

14. +342
+ -247

15.   -76
+ +38

16. -702
+ +644

17. +164
+   -84

18. -226
+ +103

19. -372
+ -104

20. - 92
+ +21

21. +122
+   -87

22. +349
+   -52

23. -472
+ -304

24. +88
+ +64

25. -72
+ -31

Name: _____ Date: _____

Subtraction of Integers

In learning to subtract integers, it is important to review the subtraction process. When you subtract two numbers, you are <u>finding the difference</u>. The numbers subtracted have special names. The first number in the subtraction problem is called the **minuend**, and the second number in the subtraction problem is called the **subtrahend**. The answer is called the **difference**. If you subtract 8 – 5, the <u>minuend</u> is 8 and the <u>subtrahend</u> is 5 with a <u>difference</u> of 3.

$$
\begin{array}{rl}
8 & \text{minuend} \\
- \ 5 & \text{subtrahend} \\
\hline
3 & \text{difference}
\end{array}
$$

In learning to subtract integers, it is important to review the method for checking subtraction. When checking subtraction, think: the subtrahend + what number = the minuend. In the above example, think: 5 + 3 = 8. Be sure to check your work as you learn to subtract integers.

Let's look at the two examples below.

Subtract
$$
\begin{array}{r}
+8 \\
- \ +6 \\
\hline
2
\end{array}
$$
You must first think, what number added to +6 will yield 8?

6 + _2_ = 8

Subtract
$$
\begin{array}{r}
-12 \\
- \ \ -4 \\
\hline
-8
\end{array}
$$
Think, what number added to -4 will yield -12?

-4 + _-8_ = -12

- -

The number line can help us understand subtraction of integers. When using the number line, it is important to check the subtraction.

When using the number line, always begin at 0. Subtracting 8 – 5, you first begin at 0, and since 8 is positive, move 8 places to the right. Then, to subtract 5, move 5 places to the left from +8 to +3 on the number line.

Step 1: move 8 places to the right of 0.

Step 2: move 5 places to the left of +8.

```
                    +8
   ──────────────────────────────────►

                        -5
            ◄──────────────
```

. . . -12 -11 -10 -9 -8 -7 -6 -5 -4 -3 -2 -1 0 +1 +2 +3 +4 +5 +6 +7 +8 +9 +10 +11 +12 . . .

Subtract -4 from -12 or
$$
\begin{array}{r}
-12 \\
- \ \ -4
\end{array}
$$
. First begin at 0 and move -12 places to the left. Think, -4 + -8 = -12. This tells us that the correct answer is -8, so the arrow moves back from -12 a total of -4 places to -8.

```
        -12
◄──────────────────

        -4
   ──────────►
```

Step 1: move 12 places to the left of 0.

Step 2: move 4 places to the right of -12.

. . . -12 -11 -10 -9 -8 -7 -6 -5 -4 -3 -2 -1 0 +1 +2 +3 +4 +5 +6 +7 +8 +9 +10 +11 +12 . . .

Name: _____ Date: _____

Subtraction of Integers: Rule/Exercises

The number line can help you understand the subtraction of positive and negative integers. However, there is a rule for subtracting positive and negative integers that can be used in solving problems.

> *Rule:* *When subtracting integers, mentally change the sign of the subtrahend and add the result to the minuend.*

Example:	-6 minuend	Mentally change the sign of the subtrahend
	– -4 subtrahend	from -4 to +4 and add to the minuend -6.
	-2	

Directions: Subtract.

1. -8 minuend   -8   Check: $2 + \underline{\hspace{1cm}} = -8$
   – +2 subtrahend ⟶ + -2
      (mentally change sign of subtrahend and add)

2. -7 minuend   -7   Check: $-4 + \underline{\hspace{1cm}} = -7$
   – -4 subtrahend ⟶ + +4
      (mentally change sign and add)

3. -10   -10   Check: $-5 + \underline{\hspace{1cm}} = -10$
   – -5 ⟶ + +5

4. +8   +8   Check: $3 + \underline{\hspace{1cm}} = +8$
   – +3 ⟶ + -3

5. -4   -4   Check: $-8 + \underline{\hspace{1cm}} = -4$
   – -8 ⟶ + +8

6. +10   +10   Check: $-10 + \underline{\hspace{1cm}} = +10$
   – -10 ⟶ + +10

7. -5   -5   Check: $-4 + \underline{\hspace{1cm}} = -5$
   – -4 ⟶ + +4

Name: _____ Date: _____

Addition and Subtraction of Integers: Exercises

Directions: Solve these problems (watch the sign that tells you to add or subtract).

1.
$$\begin{array}{r} +3 \\ + \ +5 \\ \hline \end{array}$$

2.
$$\begin{array}{r} +10 \\ + \ \ +4 \\ \hline \end{array}$$

3.
$$\begin{array}{r} -8 \\ + \ -3 \\ \hline \end{array}$$

4.
$$\begin{array}{r} -10 \\ - \ \ +9 \\ \hline \end{array}$$

5.
$$\begin{array}{r} -21 \\ - \ -18 \\ \hline \end{array}$$

6.
$$\begin{array}{r} +11 \\ + \ \ -4 \\ \hline \end{array}$$

7.
$$\begin{array}{r} -7 \\ - \ -3 \\ \hline \end{array}$$

8.
$$\begin{array}{r} +12 \\ - \ \ +7 \\ \hline \end{array}$$

9.
$$\begin{array}{r} -62 \\ + \ -14 \\ \hline \end{array}$$

10.
$$\begin{array}{r} -36 \\ - \ \ +11 \\ \hline \end{array}$$

11.
$$\begin{array}{r} +12 \\ + \ +11 \\ \hline \end{array}$$

12.
$$\begin{array}{r} -18 \\ + \ -12 \\ \hline \end{array}$$

13.
$$\begin{array}{r} +6 \\ + \ -3 \\ \hline \end{array}$$

14.
$$\begin{array}{r} -6 \\ + \ -2 \\ \hline \end{array}$$

15.
$$\begin{array}{r} -8 \\ + \ +9 \\ \hline \end{array}$$

16.
$$\begin{array}{r} -26 \\ + \ +22 \\ \hline \end{array}$$

17.
$$\begin{array}{r} -14 \\ - \ \ -5 \\ \hline \end{array}$$

18.
$$\begin{array}{r} -110 \\ + \ -214 \\ \hline \end{array}$$

$$\begin{array}{r} +21 \\ + \ -7 \\ \hline \end{array}$$
$$\begin{array}{r} -8 \\ \approx \ +9 \\ \hline \end{array}$$
$$\begin{array}{r} +55 \\ + \ -26 \\ \hline \end{array}$$
$$\begin{array}{r} -100 \\ \square \ +101 \\ \hline \end{array}$$
$$\begin{array}{r} +210 \\ + \ -189 \\ \hline \end{array}$$

Name: _____ Date: _____

Multiplication of Integers

When you multiply two numbers, the answer is called the **product**. In the rules that follow, the "product" means the answer.

There are two rules you must know to multiply integers.

Rule 1: When multiplying two numbers with the same sign, the product is positive.

Rule 2: When multiplying two numbers with different signs, the product is negative.

Directions: Use the above rules to answer the following questions.

1. +3 • +6 = +18   Which rule applies? _____

2. -3 • -6 = +18   Which rule applies? _____

3. -3 • +6 = -18   Which rule applies? _____

4. +3 • -6 = -18   Which rule applies? _____

Directions: Solve the following (multiply).

5. -2 • -4 = _____

6. +3 • -7 = _____

7. +6 • +5 = _____

8. +8 • +6 = _____

9. -9 • -8 = _____

10. +9 • +8 = _____

11. -10 • +4 = _____

12. -12 • -3 = _____

13. -11 • -8 = _____

14. -7 • +7 = _____

15. +5 • -5 = _____

16. +14 • -3 = _____

Directions: Multiply.

17.   +24
    x   -6

18.   -12
    x   -3

19.   -26
    x   +11

20.   +15
    x   +12

Name: _____ Date: _____

Division of Integers

When you divide one number by another, the first number is the **dividend** and the second number is the **divisor**. The answer or number obtained when dividing one number by another is called the **quotient**.

If 28 is divided by 4, the answer is 7, so

$$\frac{28}{4} \begin{matrix} \text{dividend} \\ \text{divisor} \end{matrix} = 7 \text{ quotient} \quad \text{or} \quad 4\overline{)28} \begin{matrix} \leftarrow \text{quotient} \\ \leftarrow \text{dividend} \end{matrix}$$

↑ divisor

Like multiplication, the rules for dividing integers are easily applied. There are two rules to use when dividing integers.

Rule 1: When dividing two numbers with the same signs, the quotient is positive.

$$\frac{+28}{+7} = +4 \text{ or } -28 \div -7 = +4$$

Rule 2: When dividing two numbers with different signs, the quotient is negative.

$$\frac{+28}{-7} = -4 \text{ or } -28 \div +7 = -4$$

Directions: Solve the following.

1. +36 ÷ +9 = _____

2. -25 ÷ -5 = _____

3. +36 ÷ -9 = _____

4. +48 ÷ +6 = _____

5. +42 ÷ -7 = _____

6. $\dfrac{+64}{-4}$ = _____

7. -32 ÷ +8 = _____

8. $\dfrac{+16}{+4}$ = _____

9. $\dfrac{-12}{+3}$ = _____

10. +75 ÷ -5 = _____

11. -35 ÷ +7 = _____

12. $\dfrac{+45}{+5}$ = _____

13. $\dfrac{+20}{+5}$ = _____

14. -12 ÷ -3 = _____

15. $\dfrac{-21}{-3}$ = _____

Directions: Divide.

16. $4\overline{)24}$

17. $-6\overline{)-42}$

18. $3\overline{)-81}$

19. $-9\overline{)63}$

20. $-7\overline{)-77}$

Name: _____ Date: _____

Variables

In mathematics, symbols are often used to represent ideas. For example, the symbol (=) means "is equal to," the symbol (>) means "is greater than," and the symbol (<) means "is less than." The symbols ÷, +, −, and • are the operation symbols that you have used many times.

Sometimes letters are used to represent numbers, and these letters are referred to as **variables**. For example, in $3 + x = 5$, x is the letter that represents the numeral 2.

However, in $3 + x =$ ___, the x is a variable that could represent many different numerals depending on the number placed in the blank.

For example:

$3 + x = 7$	The variable, or literal number, that x stands for is 4.
$3 + x = 9$	The variable, or literal number, that x stands for is 6.
$3 + x = 50$	The variable, or literal number, that x stands for is 47.

Each of the above are **equations**. In each equation the variable is x, and the number 3 is called a **constant** because 3 represents the same value in each equation. The answer following the equal (=) sign depends on the number assigned to the variable (x). *Remember*, any letter of the alphabet can be used instead of x. Let's use the letter m for a variable.

For example, in the equation $3 + m =$ ___

$3 + m = 7$	The variable m stands for 4.
$3 + m = 9$	The variable m stands for 6.
$3 + m = 50$	The variable m stands for 47.

Directions: Solve the following addition problems. Choose a number for the variable.

1. $5 + x =$ _____ $x =$ _____ the variable is _____; the constant is _____

2. $6 + y =$ _____ $y =$ _____ the variable is _____; the constant is _____

3. $9 + m =$ _____ $m =$ _____ the variable is _____; the constant is _____

4. $17 + t =$ _____ $t =$ _____ the variable is _____; the constant is _____

5. $25 + p =$ _____ $p =$ _____ the variable is _____; the constant is _____

Name: _____ Date: _____

Variables and Multiplication

Variables can be used when multiplying numbers. In multiplication problems, the symbol (•) is used to indicate multiplication. When variables are used, the sign for multiplication is often left out. For example, "3" multiplied by the variable a will usually be shown as $3a$ rather than $3 \cdot a$. In the problem $3a$, the number "3" is the constant, and the letter a is the variable. The letter a is a variable that could stand for any number. Let's work a multiplication problem with a variable.

$5a = 25$ Think: 5 multiplied by what number equals 25? 5 times 5 = 25.
The variable a equals 5.

Directions: Solve the following multiplication problems that contain a variable.

1. $3a = 6$ $a =$ _____   the constant is _____; the variable is _____

2. $4a = 28$ $a =$ _____   the constant is _____; the variable is _____

3. $9n = 45$ $n =$ _____   the constant is _____; the variable is _____

4. $7b = 56$ $b =$ _____   the constant is _____; the variable is _____

5. $12p = 48$ $p =$ _____   the constant is _____; the variable is _____

6. $10x = 120$ $x =$ _____   the constant is _____; the variable is _____

7. $15x = 90$ $x =$ _____   the constant is _____; the variable is _____

8. $20y = 100$ $y =$ _____   the constant is _____; the variable is _____

9. $14t = 42$ $t =$ _____   the constant is _____; the variable is _____

10. $8w = 72$ $w =$ _____   the constant is _____; the variable is _____

Name: _____ Date: _____

Variables and Division/Variable Exercises

Variables often appear in division problems. When variables are used in division, you will see the problem "8 divided by m" as $8 \div m$ or $\dfrac{8}{m}$. In division problems with variables, the division process can be completed once you know what number to use for the variable. In the example, $8 \div m$ or $\dfrac{8}{m}$, let the variable stand for the number 2. Then $8 \div m$ or $\dfrac{8}{m}$ becomes $8 \div 2$ or $\dfrac{8}{2}$. Divide as you usually would. So $8 \div m$ (where $m = 2$) becomes $\dfrac{8}{2} = 4$.

Directions: Solve the following division problems with variables.

1. $14 \div b = 2$ $b =$ _____   the constant is _____; the variable is _____

2. $20 \div t = 5$ $t =$ _____   the constant is _____; the variable is _____

3. $18 \div s = 6$ $s =$ _____   the constant is _____; the variable is _____

4. $24 \div y = 4$ $y =$ _____   the constant is _____; the variable is _____

5. $36 \div y = 4$ $y =$ _____   the constant is _____; the variable is _____

6. $72 \div m = 24$ $m =$ _____   the constant is _____; the variable is _____

7. $88 \div m = 8$ $m =$ _____   the constant is _____; the variable is _____

8. $49 \div x = 7$ $x =$ _____   the constant is _____; the variable is _____

Directions: Solve the following addition, subtraction, multiplication, and division problems containing variables.

9. $7 + x = 21$ $x =$ _____   10. $9 - y = 6$ $y =$ _____   11. $8y = 32$ $y =$ _____

12. $21 + t = 43$ $t =$ _____   13. $\dfrac{48}{z} = 12$ $z =$ _____   14. $16x = 64$ $x =$ _____

15. $28 - b = 7$ $b =$ _____   16. $\dfrac{21}{b} = 3$ $b =$ _____   17. $32 + m = 50$ $m =$ _____

18. $14t = 112$ $t =$ _____   19. $9a = 81$ $a =$ _____   20. $122 + c = 182$ $c =$ _____

Name: _____ Date: _____

Exponents

You will often work with exponents in mathematics. It is important to understand exponents and how to use them. When you see a figure like 3^2, the 2 is an exponent and the 3 is called the base. The **exponent** tells you the number of times the base is to be multiplied.

For example, in 3^2 the 2 tells you to multiply the 3 two times. $3^2 = 3 \cdot 3 = 9$

Directions: Answer the following.

1. 2^3 2 is the _____   3 is the _____

2. 5^4 5 is the _____   4 is the _____

3. 10^3 3 is the _____   10 is the _____

4. 8^3 8 is the _____   3 is the _____

5. 6^4 4 is the _____   6 is the _____

6. The exponent tells you the number of times the base is to be _____.

Directions: Fill in the blanks and solve the following problems.

7. $2^2 = 2 \cdot 2 =$ _____

8. $3^2 =$ _____ $\cdot$ _____ $=$ _____

9. $2^3 =$ _____ $\cdot$ _____ $\cdot$ _____ $=$ _____

10. $4^3 =$ _____ $\cdot$ _____ $\cdot$ _____ $=$ _____

11. $5^2 =$ _____ $\cdot$ _____ $=$ _____

12. $10^3 =$ _____ $\cdot$ _____ $\cdot$ _____ $=$ _____

13. $8^3 =$ _____ $\cdot$ _____ $\cdot$ _____ $=$ _____

14. $12^2 =$ _____ $\cdot$ _____ $=$ _____

15. $5^4 =$ _____ $\cdot$ _____ $\cdot$ _____ $\cdot$ _____ $=$ _____

Name: _____ Date: _____

Exponents: Maximum Power, Minimum Space

In mathematics, when a base number has an exponent, the base number is said to be raised to the indicated power, so 2^3 is read as "2 to the third power."

> 5^2 = 5 to the second power
> 3^3 = 3 to the third power
> 9^4 = 9 to the fourth power
> 4^3 = 4 to the third power

When a number (base) is raised to a power, the number (base) is multiplied the number of times indicated by the exponent (power).

> 5^2 = 5 to the second power = $5 \cdot 5 = 25$
> 3^3 = 3 to the third power = $3 \cdot 3 \cdot 3 = 27$
> 9^4 = 9 to the fourth power = $9 \cdot 9 \cdot 9 \cdot 9 = 6{,}561$
> 4^3 = 4 to the third power = $4 \cdot 4 \cdot 4 = 64$

Directions: Fill in the blanks.

1. 5——   Five to the second power.

2. 3——   Three to the third power.

3. 9——   Nine to the second power.

4. 8——   Eight to the fourth power.

5. ___^{5} Nine to the fifth power.

6. ___^{3} Seven to the third power.

7. ___^{7} Two to the seventh power.

8. _____   Five to the zero power.

9. _____   Two to the first power.

10. _____   Seven to the zero power.

Name: _____ Date: _____

Exponents: Rules to Remember

When a base is raised to the zero power or first power, remember the following:

1. *Any base raised to the zero power equals one.* $\quad 3^0 = 1, 5^0 = 1, 10^0 = 1$
2. *Any base raised to the first power equals the base.* $\quad 3^1 = 3, 5^1 = 5, 10^1 = 10$

Directions: Solve the following.

1. $7^1 =$ _____   **3.** $10^1 =$ _____   **5.** $8^{\underline{\quad}} = 1$ **7.** $9^{\underline{\quad}} = 1$

2. $3^0 =$ _____   **4.** $4^1 =$ _____   **6.** $6^{\underline{\quad}} = 1$ **8.** $9^{\underline{\quad}} = 9$

Both negative and positive numbers can be raised to a power. For example, in 2^2, the exponent tells you to raise the positive number 2 to the second power, and in -2^2, the exponent tells you to raise the negative number -2 to the second power.

It is important to learn the following rules:
- *A positive number raised to a power will always have a positive number for an answer.*
- *A negative number raised to an even power will always have a positive number for an answer.*

> For example:
> -2^2 -2 raised to the second power = 4
> -2^4 -2 raised to the fourth power = 16
> -2^6 -2 raised to the sixth power = 64
> Remember, the even numbers are 2, 4, 6, 8, 10, 12, . . .
> In the examples above, the exponents 2, 4, and 6 are all even, so the answers are positive.

- *A negative number raised to an odd power will always have a negative number for an answer.*

> For example:
> -2^3 -2 raised to the third power = -8
> -2^5 -2 raised to the fifth power = -32
> -2^7 -2 raised to the seventh power = -128
> Remember, the odd numbers are 1, 3, 5, 7, 9, 11, . . .
> In the examples above, the exponents 3, 5, and 7 are odd, so the answers will be negative.

Directions: Solve the following.

9. $2^2 =$ _____   **12.** $-5^2 =$ _____   **15.** $7^3 =$ _____   **18.** $10^2 =$ _____

10. $3^3 =$ _____   **13.** $-2^3 =$ _____   **16.** $-4^3 =$ _____   **19.** $-10^3 =$ _____

11. $-2^2 =$ _____   **14.** $-4^2 =$ _____   **17.** $-5^3 =$ _____   **20.** $-4^5 =$ _____

Name: _____ Date: _____

Adding and Subtracting Exponents

- *If the bases are the same, exponents can be added.*

For example: $2^2 \cdot 2^2 = 4 \cdot 4 = 16$ or $2^2 \cdot 2^2 = 2^{2+2} = 2^4 = 2 \cdot 2 \cdot 2 \cdot 2 = 16$

- *If the bases are different, the exponents cannot be added.*

Directions: Solve the following.

1. $3^2 \cdot 3^3 = 3^{2+3} = 3^5 = 3 \cdot 3 \cdot 3 \cdot 3 \cdot 3 = 243$

2. $2^2 \cdot 2^3 = 2$____ = ____ = ____ $\cdot$ ____ $\cdot$ ____ $\cdot$ ____ $\cdot$ ____ = ____

3. $5^2 \cdot 5^4 =$ ____ = ____ = ____ $\cdot$ ____ $\cdot$ ____ $\cdot$ ____ $\cdot$ ____ $\cdot$ ____ = ____

4. $6^1 \cdot 6^2 =$ ____ = ____ = ____ $\cdot$ ____ $\cdot$ ____ = ____

5. $2^1 \cdot 2^1 =$ ____ = ____ = ____ $\cdot$ ____ = ____

6. $10^1 \cdot 10^1 =$ ____ = ____ = ____ $\cdot$ ____ = ____

7. $7^2 \cdot 7^1 =$ ____ = ____ = ____ $\cdot$ ____ $\cdot$ ____ = ____

8. $4^2 \cdot 4^0 =$ ____ = ____ = ____ $\cdot$ ____ = ____

9. $5^0 \cdot 5^1 =$ ____ = ____ = ____

When dividing like bases with exponents, the quotient is obtained by subtracting the exponents and showing the base with the exponent after subtraction.

In dividing to find the quotient, the exponent may be positive or negative.

Example: $4^4 \div 4^2 = \dfrac{4^4}{4^2} = 4^{4-2} = 4^2$

The dividend 4^4 has the larger exponent, so the exponent in the quotient is positive, 4^2.

Example: $5^3 \div 5^5 = \dfrac{5^3}{5^5} = 5^{3-5} = 5^{-2}$

The dividend 5^3 has the smaller exponent, so after 5 is subtracted from 3, the exponent in the quotient is negative, 5^{-2}.

Directions: Simplify the following.

10. $3^4 \div 3^2 = \dfrac{3^4}{3^2} = 3^{4-2} = 3^2$

11. $4^5 \div 4^7 = \dfrac{4^5}{4^7} = 4^{5-7} =$ ____

12. $2^5 \div 2^4 =$ ____ = ____ = ____

13. $7^4 \div 7^6 =$ ____ = ____ = ____

14. $6^5 \div 6^9 =$ ____ = ____ = ____ = ____

15. $9^3 \div 9^1 =$ ____ = ____ = ____

Multiplying Exponents

In algebra you will often see terms like the following: $(3^3)^2$ and $(2)^2(2)^3$.

Let's look at the term $(3^3)^2$.
First, think: what does the base inside the parentheses with the exponent 3 say? Three to the third power.
Second, think: what does the exponent 2 outside the parentheses say? It tells you to raise the terms inside the parentheses to the second power.
So $(3^3)^2$ is three raised to the third power raised to the second power.
(3^3) is $3 \cdot 3 \cdot 3 = 27$ $3^3 = 27$ so $(3^3)^2$ becomes $(27)^2$
Now you have 27 raised to the second power, which is $(27)^2 = 27 \cdot 27 = 729$.

There is a shorter way to solve problems like this. When you have terms like $(3^3)^2$, you can multiply the exponents. So $(3^3)^2$ becomes $3^{3 \cdot 2} = 3^6 = 3 \cdot 3 \cdot 3 \cdot 3 \cdot 3 \cdot 3 = 729$, which is the same answer as above.

Directions: Solve the following (you may use your calculator for the final answer).

1. $(2^2)^2 = 2^{2 \cdot 2} = 2^4 = 16$

2. $(2^3)^2 = 2^{\underline{\quad}} \cdot {\underline{\quad}} = 2^{\underline{\quad}} = \underline{\quad}$

3. $(3^2)^2 = 3^{\underline{\quad}} \cdot {\underline{\quad}} = \underline{\quad} = \underline{\quad}$

4. $(5^2)^2 = \underline{\quad} = \underline{\quad} = \underline{\quad}$

5. $(4^2)^2 = \underline{\quad} = \underline{\quad} = \underline{\quad}$

6. $(3^1)^2 = \underline{\quad} = \underline{\quad} = \underline{\quad}$

7. $(6^0)^2 = \underline{\quad} = \underline{\quad} = \underline{\quad}$

8. $(2^3)^3 = \underline{\quad} = \underline{\quad} = \underline{\quad}$

9. $(3^3)^2 = \underline{\quad} = \underline{\quad} = \underline{\quad}$

10. $(2^2)^3 = \underline{\quad} = \underline{\quad} = \underline{\quad}$

11. $(4^1)^2 = \underline{\quad} = \underline{\quad} = \underline{\quad}$

12. $(10^2)^2 = \underline{\quad} = \underline{\quad} = \underline{\quad}$

Name: _____ Date: _____

Zero and Negative Integer Exponents

The exponents discussed so far have been with positive integers. What happens when 0, -1, -2, -3, -4, . . . are used as exponents? For example: 10^0 2^{-3} 4^{-2} $(-4)^{-2}$

x^0	When the exponent for any base number is zero, the answer is one (1). Therefore, any number used to replace the base number (x) will equal one (1) if the exponent is zero.
	Example: $10^0 = 1$

- -

x^{-n} When the exponent for any base number is negative (x^{-n}), rewrite as a fraction $\frac{1}{x^n}$ with the numerator 1. Change the negative sign of the exponent to positive.

Example: $(-4)^{-2} = \frac{1}{-4^2} = \frac{1}{16}$

Remember, a negative number (-4) raised to an even power (^{2}) results in a positive number.

Directions: Solve the following.

1. $2^0 =$ _____

2. $5^{-2} =$ _____ $\dfrac{1}{}$ = _____ $\dfrac{1}{}$

3. $3^{-3} =$ _____ = _____

4. $10^0 =$ _____

5. $10^{-2} =$ _____

6. $-10^{-2} =$ _____

7. $20^0 =$ _____

8. $-2^2 =$ _____

9. $-7^{-2} =$ _____

Review:

10. $10^2 =$ _____

11. $4^2 =$ _____

12. $5^0 =$ _____

13. $-8^2 =$ _____

14. $10^3 =$ _____

15. $8^0 =$ _____

16. $2^{-3} =$ _____

17. $5^{-2} =$ _____

18. $(-4)^{-2} =$ _____

19. $(-3)^{-2} =$ _____

20. $6^1 =$ _____

21. $5^3 =$ _____

Directions: Complete the following.

22. $2^2 + 3^3 + 4^2 =$ _____

23. $3^0 + 5^2 + 3^2 =$ _____

24. $(-3^2) + (-4^2) - 2^3 =$ _____

25. $5^0 + 6^0 + 7^0 =$ _____

26. $6^2 \div 3^2 + 2^1 =$ _____

27. $(2^2)^3 + (3^2)^2 =$ _____

28. $2^{-2} + 3^1 + 2^{-1} =$ _____

29. $3^{-2} + 2^{-2} + 2^{-3} =$ _____

30. $-2^3 \cdot -3^2 =$ _____

Name: _____ Date: _____

Scientific Notation

Exponents are very useful when working with large numbers that have been rounded off. Such large numbers are used in many of the science courses you will be studying later. Writing extremely large numbers in simple form is known as **scientific notation**.

Let's look at how scientific notation works. Let's use the following numbers:

1   10   100   1,000   10,000   100,000

Looking closely, you can see how the above numbers are related. From left to right each number is ten times larger than the one before. For example, 10 is ten times larger than 1; 100 is ten times larger than 10; 1,000 is ten times larger than 100, and so forth.

Let's look at the above numbers written with exponents.

$$1 = 10^0 \qquad\qquad 1,000 = 10^3$$
$$10 = 10^1 \qquad\qquad 10,000 = 10^4$$
$$100 = 10^2 \qquad\qquad 100,000 = 10^5$$

A science book might tell you that the planet Mars is 36,000,000 miles from Earth. It could be said that "Mars is 36 • 1,000,000 miles from Earth." Using scientific notation, the 1,000,000 can be written as 10^6 and it can then be stated as "Mars is 36 • 10^6 miles from Earth."

Let's write a number like 88,000 using scientific notation.
$$88,000 = 88 \cdot 1,000 = 88 \cdot 10^3$$

What about 3,000?
$$3,000 = 3 \cdot 1,000 = 3 \cdot 10^3$$

Directions: Solve these using scientific notation.

1. $90,000,000 = 90 \cdot 1,000,000 = 90 \cdot 10^6$

2. $20,000,000 =$ _____ • _____ = _____ • _____

3. $48,000,000 =$ _____ • _____ = _____ • _____

4. $72,000,000 =$ _____ • _____ = _____ • _____

5. $97,000,000 =$ _____ • _____ = _____ • _____

6. $26,000 =$ _____ • _____ = _____ • _____

7. $58,000 =$ _____ • _____ = _____ • _____

8. $2,000 =$ _____ • _____ = _____ • _____

9. $300 =$ _____ • _____ = _____ • _____

10. $20,000 =$ _____ • _____ = _____ • _____

Name: _____ Date: _____

Simplifying Large Numbers With Scientific Notation

You will often see decimal numbers expressed in scientific notation. For example, 36,000,000 can be written in scientific notation as $36 \cdot 10^6$ or with a decimal as $3.6 \cdot 10^7$. The exponent indicates how many digits the decimal point is moved.

$$36 \cdot 10^6 = \quad 36 \cdot 1,000,000 = 36,000,000$$
$$3.6 \cdot 10^7 = \quad 3.6 \cdot 10,000,000 = 36,000,000$$

Here is another example:

$$88 \cdot 10^3 = \quad 88 \cdot 1,000 = 88,000$$
$$8.8 \cdot 10^4 = \quad 8.8 \cdot 10,000 = 88,000$$

Directions: Complete the following using scientific notation with decimals.

1. $72,000,000 = 7.2 \cdot$ _____ $= 7.2 \cdot$ _____

2. $48,000,000 =$ _____ $\cdot$ _____ $=$ _____ $\cdot$ _____

3. $26,000,000 =$ _____ $\cdot$ _____ $=$ _____ $\cdot$ _____

4. $3,600 = 3.6 \cdot$ _____ $=$ _____ $\cdot$ _____

5. $36,000 =$ _____ $\cdot$ _____ $=$ _____ $\cdot$ _____

6. $5,500 = 5.5 \cdot$ _____ $=$ _____ $\cdot$ _____

7. $55,000 =$ _____ $\cdot$ _____ $=$ _____ $\cdot$ _____

8. $55,000,000 =$ _____ $\cdot$ _____ $=$ _____ $\cdot$ _____

9. $2,780,000,000 = 2.78 \cdot$ _____ $=$ _____ $\cdot$ _____

10. $609,000,000,000 =$ _____ $\cdot$ _____ $=$ _____ $\cdot$ _____

$$954,500,000,000,000 = 9.545 \cdot 10^{14}$$

Name: _____ Date: _____

 Learning About Factoring

The numbers multiplied together to get a product are called **factors**. For example, all the possible numbers that can be multiplied together (factors) to get the product 18 are shown below.

18 • 1 = 18	1 • 18 = 18
9 • 2 = 18	2 • 9 = 18
6 • 3 = 18	3 • 6 = 18

1, 2, 3, 6, 9, and 18 are factors of 18.

What are the factors of 12?

1 • 12 = 12	12 • 1 = 12
2 • 6 = 12	6 • 2 = 12
3 • 4 = 12	4 • 3 = 12

The factors of 12 are 1, 2, 3, 4, 6, and 12.

Let's look at ways to find out how many factors a number has. One way to find the factors of a number is by division. To find factors, find those numbers that will divide into a number and leave a remainder of zero.

Let's factor 18 using the division method. We will begin with 18 ÷ 1, 18 ÷ 2, 18 ÷ 3, 18 ÷ 4, 18 ÷ 5, 18 ÷ 6, 18 ÷ 7, 18 ÷ 8, 18 ÷ 9.

$$1\overline{)18} \quad 2\overline{)18} \quad 3\overline{)18} \quad 4\overline{)18} \quad 5\overline{)18} \quad 6\overline{)18} \quad 7\overline{)18} \quad 8\overline{)18} \quad 9\overline{)18}$$

18	9	6	4	3	3	2	2	2
18	18	18	16	15	18	14	16	18
0R	0R	0R	2R	3R	0R	4R	2R	0R

The only factors of 18 are those divisions with a remainder of zero. Those factors are 1, 2, 3, 6, 9, and 18. All of those numbers divide into 18 with a remainder of zero.

Directions: Find the factors of the following numbers by using division.

1. **8** $1\overline{)8}$ $2\overline{)8}$ $3\overline{)8}$ $4\overline{)8}$ $5\overline{)8}$ $6\overline{)8}$ $7\overline{)8}$ $8\overline{)8}$

   List the factors   _____ _____ _____ _____

2. **9** $1\overline{)9}$ $2\overline{)9}$ $3\overline{)9}$ $4\overline{)9}$ $5\overline{)9}$ $6\overline{)9}$ $7\overline{)9}$ $8\overline{)9}$ $9\overline{)9}$

   List the factors   _____ _____ _____

3. **16** $1\overline{)16}$ $2\overline{)16}$ $3\overline{)16}$ $4\overline{)16}$ $6\overline{)16}$ $7\overline{)16}$ $8\overline{)16}$ $16\overline{)16}$

   List the factors: _____ _____ _____ _____ _____

4. **15** $1\overline{)15}$ $2\overline{)15}$ $3\overline{)15}$ $4\overline{)15}$ $5\overline{)15}$ $6\overline{)15}$ $7\overline{)15}$ $15\overline{)15}$

   List the factors: _____ _____ _____ _____

Name: _____ Date: _____

Learning About Prime Factors

A whole number greater than 1 is **prime** if no number other than 1 and the number itself can divide the number. Another way to describe a prime number is to say that a **prime number** has exactly two factors: 1 and the number. For example, the number 5 is a prime number. The only numbers that will divide into 5 and have a zero remainder are 5 and 1.

Two methods for finding prime factors are the division method and the factor tree method.

What are the prime factors for 36?

Dividing: ②|36   Factor Tree: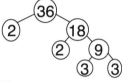
        ②|18
         ③|9
          ③

2, 2, 3, 3, are the prime factors for 36

Directions: Find the prime factors using the division method.

1. 12   2|12   Prime factors:

2. 24   2|24   Prime factors:

3. 32   2|32   Prime factors:

4. 48   2|48   Prime factors:

5. 96   2|96   Prime factors:

6. 88   2|88   Prime factors:

7. 236   2|236   Prime factors:

8. 512   2|512   Prime factors:

Name: _____ Date: _____

 Finding Prime Factors

Directions: Find the prime factors using the factor trees (show your work).

 1. 14 (14)

2. 52 (52)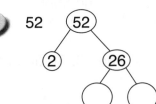

3. 90 (90)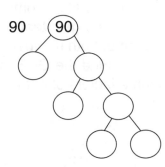

Prime factors: _____

Prime factors: _____

Prime factors: _____

4. 126 (126)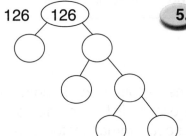

5. 342 (342)

6. 428 (428)

Prime factors: _____

Prime factors: _____

Prime factors: _____

Directions: Write each of the following numbers as a product of prime factors. Use the factor trees above.

7. 14   _____ · _____ = 14

8. 52   _____ · _____ · _____ = _____

9. 90   _____ · _____ · _____ · _____ = 90

10. 126   _____ · _____ · _____ · _____ = _____

11. 342   _____ · _____ · _____ · _____ = _____

12. 428   _____ · _____ · _____ = _____

Name: _____ Date: _____

 ## Learning About the Greatest Common Factor

Let's work with two numbers and see how they can be compared. We will be trying to find the greatest common factor for these two numbers.

The **greatest common factor (GCF)** for two numbers is the largest number that is a factor of both numbers.

Find the GCF for the numbers 24 and 18. To find the GCF, it is necessary to find the prime factors of both numbers.

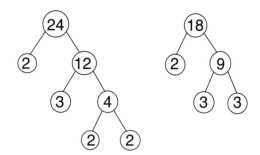

Prime factors for 24: 2 3 2 2
Prime factors for 18: 2 3 3

Circle the prime factors common to both numbers and multiply: 2 • 3 = 6

Arrange the prime factors for each number so the prime factors found in both numbers can be identified. In the box above, the prime factors 2 and 3 are found in both numbers. Multiply these two prime numbers and the answer is six. Six is the greatest common factor found in both 24 and 18.

Find the GCF for the numbers 48 and 64. First, find the prime factors for each number.

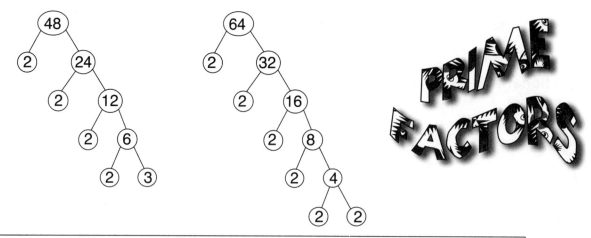

Prime factors for 48   2 2 2 2 3
Prime factors for 64   2 2 2 2 2 2

Multiply the prime factors common to both numbers: 2 • 2 • 2 • 2 = 16
16 is the GCF for 48 and 64

Name: _____ Date: _____

 Finding the Greatest Common Factor

Directions: Find the greatest common factor for the following pairs of numbers.

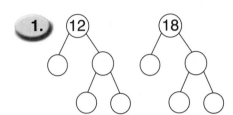

Prime for 12: _____

Prime for 18: _____

GCF: _____

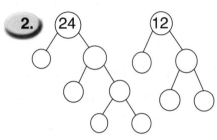

Prime for 24: _____

Prime for 12: _____

GCF: _____

 3. 36   54

Prime for 36: _____

Prime for 54: _____

GCF: _____

4. 18   30

Prime for 18: _____

Prime for 30: _____

GCF: _____

5. 18   27

Prime for 18: _____

Prime for 27: _____

GCF: _____

 6. 56   16

Prime for 56: _____

Prime for 16: _____

GCF: _____

  7. 93   69

Prime for 93: _____

Prime for 69: _____

GCF: _____

8. 72   216

Prime for 72: _____

Prime for 216: _____

GCF: _____

Name: _____ Date: _____

Learning About the Least Common Multiple

In finding the **least common multiple (LCM)**, you are trying to find the smallest non-zero number that is the multiple of two numbers. The least common multiple of two numbers is found by listing the multiples of the two numbers and then comparing to find the smallest number that is a multiple of both numbers.

Example: Find the LCM for 18 and 24.

The multiples for 18 are: $1 \cdot 18 = 18$; $2 \cdot 18 = 36$; $3 \cdot 18 = 54$; $4 \cdot 18 = 72$; $5 \cdot 18 = 90$ . . .

The multiples for 24 are: $1 \cdot 24 = 24$; $2 \cdot 24 = 48$; $3 \cdot 24 = 72$; $4 \cdot 24 = 96$; $5 \cdot 24 = 120$ . . .

Multiples for 18: 18, 36, 54, ⟨72⟩ 90	72 is the LCM for the
Multiples for 24: 24, 48, ⟨72⟩ 96, 120	numbers 18 and 24.

Directions: Find the LCM for the following pairs of numbers.

1.   5:   5, ___, ___, ___, ___, ___, ___

      7:   7, ___, ___, ___, ___, ___, ___

      LCM = _____

2.   6:   6, ___, ___, ___, ___, ___

      10: 10, ___, ___, ___, ___, ___

      LCM = _____

3.   4: _____

      10: _____

      LCM = _____

4.   14: _____

      21: _____

      LCM = _____

5.   30: _____

      45: _____

      LCM = _____

6.   15: _____

      25: _____

      LCM = _____

7.   18: _____

      20: _____

      LCM = _____

8.   6: _____

      14: _____

      LCM = _____

9.   8: _____

      34: _____

      LCM = _____

10.   12: _____

      22: _____

      LCM = _____

Name: _____ Date: _____

Radicals and Roots

In algebra you will see problems with radicals. The ($\sqrt{\ }$) is the radical sign. When you are told to find "the square root of 4," it will often be written as $\sqrt[2]{4}$ or $\sqrt{4}$. You are asked to find the numbers (roots) that, when squared, equal 4. There are two numbers (roots) that, when squared, give you 4. The numbers (roots) are 2 and -2.

$2 \cdot 2 = 4$	Two positive numbers multiplied equal +4.
$-2 \cdot -2 = 4$	Two negative numbers multiplied equal +4.

When you see $\sqrt{\ }$, it is the **radical sign**. The number under the radical is the **radicand**.

The $\sqrt{\ }$ radical sign tells you to find the square root of the radicand under the radical. $\sqrt{9}$ means "find the square root of 9."

Many times you will need to find cube roots, fourth roots, and so on. The number above the radical will tell you the root to find. The number above the radical is the **index**.

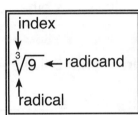

$\sqrt[2]{\ }$ or $\sqrt{\ }$ means find the square root	$\sqrt[3]{\ }$ means find the cube root
$\sqrt[4]{\ }$ means find the fourth root	$\sqrt[8]{\ }$ means find the eighth root

Directions: Complete the following.

1. Write the symbol for the radical. _____

2. The number under the radical sign is called the _____.

3. $\sqrt{4}$ or $\sqrt[2]{4}$ tells you to find the s _ _ _ _ _ r _ _ _ of f _ _ _.

4. $\sqrt[3]{8}$ tells you to find the c _ _ _ r _ _ _ of e _ _ _ _.

5. $\sqrt[4]{16}$ tells you to find the f _ _ _ _ _ r _ _ _ of s _ _ _ _ _ _.

Name: _____   Date: _____

Finding Square Roots

The radical $\sqrt[2]{4}$ or $\sqrt{4}$ asks you to find the two numbers (roots) that multiplied equal 4. The radical $\sqrt{9}$ or $\sqrt[2]{9}$ asks you to find the two numbers (roots) that multiplied equal 9.

$\sqrt[2]{4}$ or $\sqrt{4}$ $2 \cdot 2 = 4$ or $-2 \cdot -2 = 4$

2 and -2 are the numbers or roots that when multiplied equal 4.

$\sqrt[2]{9}$ or $\sqrt{9}$ $3 \cdot 3 = 9$ or $-3 \cdot -3 = 9$

3 and -3 are the numbers or roots that when multiplied equal 9.

Unless otherwise noted, find only the positive roots.

Directions: Solve the following.

1. $\sqrt{4}$ = _____   6. $\sqrt{64}$ = _____

2. $\sqrt{9}$ = _____   7. $\sqrt{100}$ = _____

3. $\sqrt{16}$ = _____   8. $\sqrt{25}$ = _____

4. $\sqrt{36}$ = _____   9. $\sqrt{81}$ = _____

5. $\sqrt{49}$ = _____   10. $\sqrt{144}$ = _____

Directions: Answer the following.

11. The square root of 4 is _____.   13. The square root of 100 is _____.

12. The square root of 36 is _____.   14. The square root of 49 is _____.

Directions: Use the <u>radical sign</u> and write the problem that would tell you to find the following.

15. The square root of 9 ___$\sqrt{9}$___   18. The square root of 25 _____

16. The square root of 64 ___$\sqrt{}$___   19. The square root of 144 _____

17. The square root of 81 _____   20. The square root of 16 _____

Name: _____ Date: _____

Adding Radicals

Radicals can be added. When adding radicals, the radicals must have the <u>same</u> index and the <u>same</u> radicand.

$2\sqrt{3} + 3\sqrt{3}$ can be added because the radicands are the same (3), and the index in both is square root (2).

$$2\overset{\downarrow\ \text{index}\ \downarrow}{\sqrt{3}} + 3\underset{\uparrow\ \text{radicand}\ \uparrow}{\sqrt{3}}$$

$2\sqrt{3} + 2\sqrt[3]{5}$ cannot be added because the radicands are different (3 and 5), and the indexes (2 and 3) are different.

---

coefficients: ↓   ↓

Add: $2\sqrt{3} + 3\sqrt{3}$

Step 1: Add the coefficients 2 and 3. $2 + 3 = 5$

Step 2: Rewrite the answer as $5\sqrt{3}$

$$2\sqrt{3} + 3\sqrt{3} = (2+3)\sqrt{3} = 5\sqrt{3}$$

Directions: Add the following.

1. $7\sqrt{2} + 3\sqrt{2} = (7+3)\sqrt{2} = \underline{\ \ }\sqrt{2}$

2. $4\sqrt{5} + 3\sqrt{5} = (\underline{\ \ } + \underline{\ \ })\sqrt{5} = \underline{\ \ }\sqrt{5}$

3. $2\sqrt{7} + 4\sqrt{7} + 3\sqrt{7} = (\underline{\ \ } + \underline{\ \ } + \underline{\ \ })\sqrt{7} = \underline{\ \ }\sqrt{7}$

4. $10\sqrt{3} + 8\sqrt{3} + 2\sqrt{3} = (\underline{\ \ } + \underline{\ \ } + \underline{\ \ })\sqrt{\underline{\ \ }} = \underline{\ \ }\sqrt{\underline{\ \ }}$

5. $9\sqrt{5} + 5\sqrt{5} = (\underline{\ \ } + \underline{\ \ })\sqrt{\underline{\ \ }} = \underline{\ \ }\sqrt{\underline{\ \ }}$

6. $7\sqrt{29} + 14\sqrt{29} + 2\sqrt{29} = \underline{\hspace{3cm}}$

7. $14\sqrt{31} + 6\sqrt{31} + 5\sqrt{31} = \underline{\hspace{3cm}}$

When the radical appears without a coefficient before it, the coefficient is the number 1.

$$\sqrt{3} = 1\sqrt{3} \qquad \text{Add: } 3\overset{\downarrow\ \text{coefficient 3}}{\sqrt{2}} + \underset{\uparrow\text{coefficient 1}}{\sqrt{2}} = (3+1)\sqrt{2} = 4\sqrt{2}$$

8. $\sqrt{5} + 2\sqrt{5} = (\underline{\ \ } + \underline{\ \ })\sqrt{5} = \underline{\ \ }\sqrt{5}$

9. $3\sqrt{22} + 19\sqrt{22} + \sqrt{22} = (\underline{\ \ } + \underline{\ \ } + \underline{\ \ })\sqrt{22} = \underline{\ \ }\sqrt{22}$

10. $8\sqrt{7} + \sqrt{7} + 4\sqrt{7} = \underline{\hspace{3cm}}$

Name: _____ Date: _____

Subtracting Radicals

When subtracting radicals, the radicals subtracted must have the <u>same</u> radicands and the <u>same</u> indexes.

$5\sqrt{3} - 3\sqrt{3}$ can be subtracted because the radicands are the same (3) and the indexes are the same (2).

$$\downarrow \text{ index } \downarrow$$
$$2\sqrt{3} + 3\sqrt{3}$$
$$\uparrow \text{ radicand } \uparrow$$

$5\sqrt{3} - 3\sqrt[3]{3}$ cannot be subtracted because the indexes are different (2 and 3).

> Subtract: $5\sqrt{3} - 3\sqrt{3}$
> **Step 1:** Subtract the coefficients. $5 - 3 = 2$
> **Step 2:** Rewrite the answer as $2\sqrt{3}$
> $$5\sqrt{3} - 3\sqrt{3} = (5-3)\sqrt{3} = 2\sqrt{3}$$

Directions: Subtract the following.

1. $8\sqrt{5} - 3\sqrt{5} = (8 - \underline{\quad})\sqrt{5} = \underline{\quad}\sqrt{5}$

2. $14\sqrt{11} - 7\sqrt{11} = (\underline{\quad} - \underline{\quad})\sqrt{\underline{\quad}} = \underline{\quad}\sqrt{\underline{\quad}}$

3. $32\sqrt{7} - 15\sqrt{7} = (\underline{\quad} - \underline{\quad})\sqrt{\underline{\quad}} = \underline{\quad}\sqrt{\underline{\quad}}$

4. $5\sqrt{31} - 2\sqrt{31} - \sqrt{31} = (\underline{\quad} - \underline{\quad} - \underline{\quad})\sqrt{\underline{\quad}} = \underline{\quad}\sqrt{\underline{\quad}}$

5. $8\sqrt{15} - 10\sqrt{15} = (\underline{\quad} - \underline{\quad})\sqrt{\underline{\quad}} = -2\sqrt{\underline{\quad}}$

6. $7\sqrt{3} - 11\sqrt{3} = (\underline{\quad} - \underline{\quad})\sqrt{\underline{\quad}} = -\underline{\quad}\sqrt{\underline{\quad}}$

7. $26\sqrt{8} - 5\sqrt{8} - 23\sqrt{8} = (\underline{\quad} - \underline{\quad} - \underline{\quad})\sqrt{\underline{\quad}} = -\underline{\quad}\sqrt{\underline{\quad}}$

8. $4\sqrt{6} - 3\sqrt{6} = \underline{\hspace{3cm}}$

9. $27\sqrt{41} - 22\sqrt{41} = \underline{\hspace{3cm}}$

Directions: Solve the following. Watch the signs!

10. $10\sqrt{3} + 8\sqrt{3} - 5\sqrt{3} = (\underline{\quad} + \underline{\quad} - \underline{\quad})\sqrt{\underline{\quad}} = \underline{\quad}\sqrt{\underline{\quad}}$

11. $27\sqrt{5} - 13\sqrt{5} + 2\sqrt{5} - 8\sqrt{5} = (\underline{\quad} - \underline{\quad} + \underline{\quad} - \underline{\quad})\sqrt{\underline{\quad}} = \underline{\quad}\sqrt{\underline{\quad}}$

12. $14\sqrt{11} - 18\sqrt{11} + 2\sqrt{11} = (\underline{\quad} - \underline{\quad} + \underline{\quad})\sqrt{\underline{\quad}} = -\underline{\quad}\sqrt{\underline{\quad}}$

Name: _____ Date: _____

Multiplying and Dividing Radicals

Multiply radicals as you would whole numbers. When multiplying radicals, the indexes must be the same; however, the radicands can be different.

$$\sqrt{3} \cdot \sqrt{3} \quad \text{think } 3 \cdot 3 = 9 \text{ so} \sqrt{3} \cdot \sqrt{3} = \sqrt{9} = 3$$
$$\sqrt{2} \cdot \sqrt{8} \quad \text{think } 2 \cdot 8 = 16 \text{ so} \sqrt{2} \cdot \sqrt{8} = \sqrt{16} = 4$$

Directions: Solve the following.

1. $\sqrt{3} \cdot \sqrt{3} = \sqrt{\underline{}} = \underline{}$

2. $\sqrt[4]{2} \cdot \sqrt[4]{8} = \sqrt[4]{\underline{}} = \underline{}$

3. $\sqrt{4} \cdot \sqrt{4} = \sqrt{\underline{}} = \underline{}$

4. $\sqrt{2} \cdot \sqrt{2} = \sqrt{\underline{}} = \underline{}$

5. $\sqrt{7} \cdot \sqrt{7} = \sqrt{\underline{}} = \underline{}$

6. $\sqrt{4} \cdot \sqrt{16} = \sqrt{\underline{}} = \underline{}$

7. $\sqrt[3]{9} \cdot \sqrt[3]{3} = \sqrt[3]{\underline{}} = \underline{}$

8. $\sqrt{4} \cdot \sqrt{9} = \sqrt{\underline{}} = \underline{}$

9. $\sqrt{5} \cdot \sqrt{5} = \sqrt{\underline{}} = \underline{}$

10. $\sqrt{10} \cdot \sqrt{10} = \sqrt{\underline{}} = \underline{}$

Divide radicals as you would divide whole numbers. When dividing radicals, the indexes must be the same; however, the radicands can be different.

$$\frac{\sqrt{12}}{\sqrt{3}} \quad \text{think} \quad \frac{12}{3} = 4 \quad \text{so} \quad \frac{\sqrt{12}}{\sqrt{3}} = \sqrt{4} = 2$$

Directions: Solve the following.

11. $\dfrac{\sqrt{36}}{\sqrt{9}} = \sqrt{4} = \underline{}$

12. $\dfrac{\sqrt[3]{64}}{\sqrt[3]{8}} = \sqrt[3]{8} = \underline{}$

13. $\dfrac{\sqrt{27}}{\sqrt{3}} = \sqrt{\underline{}} = \underline{}$

14. $\dfrac{\sqrt{75}}{\sqrt{3}} = \sqrt{\underline{}} = \underline{}$

15. $\dfrac{\sqrt[5]{96}}{\sqrt[5]{3}} = \sqrt[5]{\underline{}} = \underline{}$

16. $\dfrac{\sqrt{50}}{\sqrt{2}} = \sqrt{\underline{}} = \underline{}$

17. $\dfrac{\sqrt[3]{81}}{\sqrt[3]{3}} = \sqrt[3]{\underline{}} = \underline{}$

18. $\dfrac{\sqrt{64}}{\sqrt{16}} = \sqrt{\underline{}} = \underline{}$

19. $\dfrac{\sqrt[4]{3,125}}{\sqrt[4]{5}} = \sqrt[4]{\underline{}} = \underline{}$

20. $\dfrac{\sqrt{24}}{\sqrt{6}} = \sqrt{\underline{}} = \underline{}$

Name: _____ Date: _____

Simplifying Radicals

Many radicals can be changed to an equivalent form that is easier to use in solving problems. Changing a radical to this new form is called <u>simplifying</u>.

Step 1: To simplify $\sqrt{18}$, think $\sqrt{18} = \sqrt{2 \cdot 9}$

Step 2: $\sqrt{2 \cdot 9}$ can be written as $\sqrt{2} \cdot \sqrt{9}$

Step 3: Find the $\sqrt{9} = 3$ and rewrite as $3 \cdot \sqrt{2}$ or $3\sqrt{2}$

So $\sqrt{18} = \sqrt{9 \cdot 2} = \sqrt{9} \cdot \sqrt{2} = 3 \cdot \sqrt{2} = 3\sqrt{2}$

Directions: Simplify the following.

1. $\sqrt{12} = \sqrt{4 \cdot \underline{\quad}} = \sqrt{4} \cdot \sqrt{\underline{\quad}} = 2 \cdot \sqrt{\underline{\quad}} = 2\sqrt{\underline{\quad}}$

2. $\sqrt{18} = \sqrt{9 \cdot \underline{\quad}} = \sqrt{9} \cdot \sqrt{\underline{\quad}} = 3 \cdot \sqrt{\underline{\quad}} = \underline{\quad}\sqrt{\underline{\quad}}$

3. $\sqrt{20} = \sqrt{\underline{\quad} \cdot \underline{\quad}} = \sqrt{\underline{\quad}} \cdot \sqrt{\underline{\quad}} = \underline{\quad} \cdot \sqrt{\underline{\quad}} = \underline{\quad}\sqrt{\underline{\quad}}$

4. $\sqrt{27} = \sqrt{\underline{\quad} \cdot \underline{\quad}} = \sqrt{\underline{\quad}} \cdot \sqrt{\underline{\quad}} = \underline{\quad} \cdot \sqrt{\underline{\quad}} = \underline{\quad}\sqrt{\underline{\quad}}$

5. $\sqrt{8} = \sqrt{\underline{\quad} \cdot \underline{\quad}} = \sqrt{\underline{\quad}} \cdot \sqrt{\underline{\quad}} = \underline{\quad} \cdot \sqrt{\underline{\quad}} = \underline{\quad}\sqrt{\underline{\quad}}$

6. $\sqrt{24} = \sqrt{4 \cdot \underline{\quad}} = \sqrt{\underline{\quad}} \cdot \sqrt{\underline{\quad}} = \underline{\quad} \cdot \sqrt{\underline{\quad}} = \underline{\quad}\sqrt{\underline{\quad}}$

7. $\sqrt{32} = \sqrt{4 \cdot \underline{\quad}} = \underline{\hspace{2cm}} = \underline{\hspace{2cm}} = \underline{\hspace{2cm}}$

8. $\sqrt{50} = \sqrt{\underline{\quad} \cdot 2} = \underline{\hspace{2cm}} = \underline{\hspace{2cm}} = \underline{\hspace{2cm}}$

9. $\sqrt{48} = \sqrt{\underline{\quad} \cdot 3} = \underline{\hspace{2cm}} = \underline{\hspace{2cm}} = \underline{\hspace{2cm}}$

10. $\sqrt{45} = \sqrt{9 \cdot \underline{\quad}} = \underline{\hspace{2cm}} = \underline{\hspace{2cm}} = \underline{\hspace{2cm}}$

Review: Write the square root of each of the following.

11. $16 = \underline{\quad}$

13. $36 = \underline{\quad}$

15. $9 = \underline{\quad}$

17. $144 = \underline{\quad}$

12. $49 = \underline{\quad}$

14. $25 = \underline{\quad}$

16. $100 = \underline{\quad}$

18. $64 = \underline{\quad}$

Name: _____ Date: _____

  # Multiplying and Simplifying Radicals

Directions: Multiply the radicals in the following exercise. After multiplying the radicals, simplify.

> ***Example:***   Multiply and simplify $\sqrt{12} \cdot \sqrt{2}$
>   **Step 1:** multiply $\sqrt{12} \cdot \sqrt{2} = \sqrt{24}$
>   **Step 2:** simplify $\sqrt{24} = \sqrt{4} \cdot \sqrt{6} = 2 \cdot \sqrt{6} = 2\sqrt{6}$

1. $\sqrt{3} \cdot \sqrt{15} = \sqrt{\underline{\quad}} = \sqrt{\underline{\ }} \cdot \sqrt{5} = \underline{\quad} \cdot \sqrt{\underline{\ }} = \underline{\quad}\sqrt{\underline{\ }}$

2. $\sqrt{2} \cdot \sqrt{6} = \sqrt{\underline{\quad}} = \sqrt{\underline{\ }} \cdot \sqrt{3} = \underline{\quad} \cdot \sqrt{\underline{\ }} = \underline{\quad}\sqrt{\underline{\ }}$

3. $\sqrt{3} \cdot \sqrt{6} = \sqrt{\underline{\quad}} = \sqrt{\underline{\ }} \cdot \sqrt{\underline{\ }} = \underline{\quad} \cdot \sqrt{\underline{\ }} = \underline{\quad}\sqrt{\underline{\ }}$

4. $\sqrt{3} \cdot \sqrt{8} = \sqrt{\underline{\quad}} = \sqrt{\underline{\ }} \cdot \sqrt{\underline{\ }} = \underline{\quad} \cdot \sqrt{\underline{\ }} = \underline{\quad}\sqrt{\underline{\ }}$

5. $\sqrt{2} \cdot \sqrt{14} = \sqrt{\underline{\quad}} = \sqrt{\underline{\ }} \cdot \sqrt{\underline{\ }} = \underline{\quad} \cdot \sqrt{\underline{\ }} = \underline{\quad}\sqrt{\underline{\ }}$

Dividing and Simplifying Radicals

Directions: Divide the radicals in the following exercises. After dividing the radicals, simplify.

> ***Example:***   Divide and simplify $\sqrt{24} \div \sqrt{3}$
>   **Step 1:** Divide $\sqrt{24} \div \sqrt{3} = \dfrac{\sqrt{24}}{\sqrt{3}} = \sqrt{8}$
>   **Step 2:** Simplify $\sqrt{8} = \sqrt{4} \cdot \sqrt{2} = 2 \cdot \sqrt{2} = 2\sqrt{2}$

1. $\dfrac{\sqrt{32}}{\sqrt{4}} = \sqrt{\underline{\ }} = \sqrt{\underline{\ }} \cdot \sqrt{\underline{\ }} = \underline{\quad} \cdot \sqrt{\underline{\ }} = \underline{\quad}\sqrt{\underline{\ }}$

2. $\dfrac{\sqrt{48}}{\sqrt{4}} = \sqrt{\underline{\ }} = \sqrt{\underline{\ }} \cdot \sqrt{\underline{\ }} = \underline{\quad} \cdot \sqrt{\underline{\ }} = \underline{\quad}\sqrt{\underline{\ }}$

3. $\dfrac{\sqrt{64}}{\sqrt{2}} = \sqrt{\underline{\ }} = \sqrt{\underline{\ }} \cdot \sqrt{\underline{\ }} = \underline{\quad} \cdot \sqrt{\underline{\ }} = \underline{\quad}\sqrt{\underline{\ }}$

4. $\dfrac{\sqrt{56}}{\sqrt{2}} = \sqrt{\underline{\ }} = \sqrt{\underline{\ }} \cdot \sqrt{\underline{\ }} = \underline{\quad} \cdot \sqrt{\underline{\ }} = \underline{\quad}\sqrt{\underline{\ }}$

Name: _____ Date: _____

Learning About Simple Equations

Many of the math problems you will solve involve equations. **Equations** are mathematical statements that two expressions are equal.

> $5 + y = 7$ is an equation.
> $5 + y$ is one **member** of the equation.
> 7 is one member of the equation.
> The equal (=) sign tells you the expressions are equal.

In solving equations, you will be solving for the unknown. The **unknown** in the above equation is y. Replace y with the number that, added to 5, equals 7.

> $5 + y = 7$ Find a number for y.
> $5 + 2 = 7$ Substitute the number 2 for y. Add.
> $7 = 7$

The number 2 is the correct number for y since $7 = 7$ is correct. The number 2 is the **solution** to the above question.

In equations like $5 + y = 7$ or $7 - x = 4$, the letters y and x are unknowns. Letters such as y and x are used in equations to represent the unknown. These letters are called **variables**.

In solving equations like $5 + y = 7$, you can subtract the same number from each *member* of the equation, and the resulting equation will still be equal. This is very important in helping you solve such problems. The subtraction process undoes the addition. *Subtraction is the opposite of addition*. Subtraction and addition are inverse operations because they are opposites.

> $5 + y = 7$ <u>Subtract</u> 5 from each member of the equation.
> $5 + y - 5 = 7 - 5$
> $0 + y = 2$ Subtracting 5 from both members of the equation
> $y = 2$ helps you find the number y equals.

Name: _____   Date: _____

Finding the Value of the Unknown—I

Directions: Solve each problem as directed.

Find the unknown.

1. $y + 4 = 9$ Solve by subtracting 4 from each member of the equation.

$y + 4 - 4 = 9 - 4$ $y + 0 = 5$ $y = 5$

Check by substituting the solution for y. $5 + 4 = 9$

2. $x + 10 = 21$ Solve by subtracting 10 from each member of the equation.

$x + 10 -$ ____ $= 21 -$ ____ $x +$ ____ $=$ ____ $x =$ ____

Check by substituting the solution for x.   ____ $+ 10 = 21$

3. $v + 17 = 28$ Solve by subtracting 17 from each member of the equation.

$v + 17 -$ ____ $= 28 -$ ____ $v +$ ____ $=$ ____ $v =$ ____

Check by substituting the solution for v.   ____ $+ 17 = 28$

Find the unknown. Check your solution.

4. $t + 8 = 16$ **7.** $n + 72 = 101$ **10.** $y + 8 = 32$

5. $w + 19 = 25$ **8.** $y + 16 = 29$ **11.** $z + 12 = 30$

6. $b + 34 = 51$ **9.** $x + 3 = 27$ **12.** $x + 41 = 90$

Write the equation.

13. If you add 12 to a number, the sum is 26. Think: what is the unknown? If the unknown is added to 12, the sum is 26. Choose a letter for the unknown and write the equation.

____ $+$ ____ $= 26$

Name: _____ Date: _____

 # Finding the Value of the Unknown—II

Many times you will be asked to find the unknown in an equation where a number is subtracted from the unknown.

For example: $x - 7 = 10$

In equations like $x - 7 = 10$, you can <u>add</u> the same number to each member of the equation, and the resulting equation will still be equal.

$x - 7 = 10$	Add +7 to each member of the equation.
$x - 7 + 7 = 10 + 7$	
$x + 0 = 17$	Adding +7 to each member of the equation
$x = 17$	helps you find the number x equals.

The addition of +7 is the opposite of the -7. Adding +7 undoes the subtraction of -7. *Addition is the inverse operation of subtraction because it has an opposite effect.*

Directions: Solve each problem as directed.

Find the unknown.

1. $y - 3 = 18$ Solve by adding +3 to each member of the equation.

$y - 3 +$ ____ $= 18 +$ ____ $y +$ ____ $=$ ____ $y =$ ____

Check by substituting the solution for y. ____ $- 3 = 18$

2. $x - 5 = 20$ Solve by adding +5 to each member of the equation.

$x - 5 +$ ____ $= 20 +$ ____ $x +$ ____ $=$ ____ $x =$ ____

Check by substituting the solution for x. ____ $- 5 = 20$

Find the unknown. Check the solution.

3. $b - 12 = 7$ **6.** $v - 7 = -3$ **9.** $x - 5 = 4$

4. $t - 4 = 8$ **7.** $y - 4 = -1$ **10.** $t - 8 = -12$

5. $w - 11 = 3$ **8.** $x - 10 = 3$ **11.** $y - 7 = 11$

Name: _____ Date: _____

Reviewing Simple Equations

Directions: Complete the following.

1. Equations are _____ statements with _____ expressions that are equal.

2. In the equation $x + 4 = 9$, the two members of the equation are _____ and _____.

3. In solving equations, you can add or _____ the same number from each member of the equation without changing the result.

> The fact that you can add the same number to each side of an equation without changing the results of the equation has a special name. It is known as the *addition principle of equations.*
>
> The fact that you can subtract the same number from each member of the equation without changing the result has a special name. It is known as the *subtraction principle of equations.*

Directions: Write equations for these problems and solve for the unknown.

4. Aaron bought an apple for 38 cents and had 26 cents left over. How much money did he have before buying the apple?

   a. Think: The unknown is the amount of money Aaron had before he bought the apple.

      Choose a letter to be the unknown. What letter did you choose? _____

   b. Think: What number must be subtracted from the unknown? _____

   c. Complete the equation. _____ – _____ = 26

   d. How much money did Aaron have before he bought the apple? _____

   e. Check your answer on your own paper. Show your work.

5. Evan made 12 free throws, helping his team win the game. If he had made 6 more free throws, he would have made as many as the total team. How many free throws did Evan's team make? Write the equation and solve the problem.

_____

Name: _____ Date: _____

Solving Equations With Multiplication

Many equations involve multiplication. An equation with multiplication would be $2n = 6$ ($2n$ is another way to write $2 \cdot n$). $2n = 6$ asks "2 times what number (unknown) = 6?"

In solving equations with multiplication, you want to undo the multiplication. *Division is the opposite, or inverse, operation of multiplication* and can be used to solve this problem.

$2n = 6$ To find n, each member of the equation can be divided by the same number without changing the result.

$\dfrac{2n}{2} = \dfrac{6}{2}$ Divide each member of the equation by 2.

$\dfrac{2n}{2} = n$ $\dfrac{6}{2} = 3$ (Remember, $\frac{2}{2} = 1$, but you usually do not place the 1 before the unknown.)

$n = 3$ Rewrite the equation.

Now check your work by substituting 3 for n in the original equation.
$2n = 6$ becomes $2 \cdot 3 = 6$ $6 = 6$

Even though you write $2n$ without the multiplication sign ($\cdot$), when two numbers are written together, use ($\cdot$) between them to indicate multiplication.

Directions: Find the unknown (check each problem).

1. $8x = 16$ Divide each member by 8.

$\dfrac{8x}{8} = \dfrac{16}{8}$ _____ = _____

Substitute the number x equals to check.

$8 \cdot$ _____ $= 16$

2. $14x = 28$

$\dfrac{14x}{} = \dfrac{28}{}$ _____ = _____

$14 \cdot$ _____ $= 28$

3. $8x = 24$

$\dfrac{8x}{} = \dfrac{24}{}$ _____ = _____

$8 \cdot$ _____ $= 24$

4. $12x = 60$ $x =$ _____

5. $12y = 36$ $y =$ _____

6. $4t = 32$ $t =$ _____

7. $24w = 48$ $w =$ _____

8. $18p = 36$ $p =$ _____

9. $4t = 16$ $t =$ _____

10. $5t = 55$ $t =$ _____

11. $12y = 144$ $y =$ _____

12. $2e = 16$ $e =$ _____

13. $8r = 32$ $r =$ _____

14. $3x = 42$ $x =$ _____

15. $6y = 60$ $y =$ _____

Name: _____ Date: _____

Solving Equations With Division

Many equations involve division. Equations like $\frac{x}{12} = 4$ tell you that the unknown x divided by 12 equals 4. When solving equations with division, you must first undo the division. *Multiplication is the inverse, or opposite, operation of division.* To undo the division in $\frac{x}{12} = 4$, each member of the equation can be multiplied by the same number without changing the results.

$\frac{x}{12} = 4$	Multiplication will undo division, so find a number that can be multiplied by both members of the equation.
$\frac{x}{12} \cdot 12 = 4 \cdot 12$	Multiply both members of the equation by 12.
$\frac{x}{\cancel{12}} \cdot \cancel{12} = 48$	The two 12s in the left member cancel each other, and you must multiply $4 \cdot 12$ in the right member.
$x = 48$	
$\frac{48}{12} = 4$	Check by substituting the solution (48) for x in the
$4 = 4$	equation and complete the division.

Directions: Find the unknown (check each problem).

1. $\frac{y}{4} = 6$ Undo the division by multiplying each member of the equation by 4.

$\frac{y}{4} \cdot$ _____ $= 6 \cdot$ _____   _____ $=$ _____

$\frac{}{4} = 6$ Substitute the number y equals in the equation and check.

_____ $= 6$

2. $\frac{x}{2} = 7$ Undo the division by multiplying each member of the equation by 2.

$\frac{x}{2} \cdot$ _____ $= 7 \cdot$ _____   _____ $=$ _____

$\frac{}{2} = 7$ Substitute the number x equals in the equation and check.

_____ $= 7$

Name: _____ Date: _____

Solving Equations With Division *(continued)*

3. $\dfrac{t}{5} = 6$ $\dfrac{t}{5} \cdot$ ___ $= 6 \cdot$ ___   ___ = ___   Check: $\dfrac{}{5} = 6$ ___ = 6

4. $\dfrac{w}{8} = 4$ $\dfrac{w}{8} \cdot$ ___ $= 4 \cdot$ ___   ___ = ___   Check: $\dfrac{}{8} = 4$ ___ = ___

5. $\dfrac{p}{9} = 8$ $\dfrac{p}{9} \cdot$ ___ $= 8 \cdot$ ___   ___ = ___   Check: $\dfrac{}{9} = 8$ ___ = ___

6. $\dfrac{x}{3} = 12$ $\dfrac{x}{3} \cdot$ ___ $= 12 \cdot$ ___   ___ = ___   Check: $\dfrac{}{3} = 12$ ___ = ___

7. $\dfrac{y}{12} = 12$ $\dfrac{y}{12} \cdot$ ___ $= 12 \cdot$ ___   ___ = ___   Check: $\dfrac{}{12} = 12$ ___ = ___

8. $\dfrac{c}{16} = 4$ $\dfrac{c}{16} \cdot$ ___ $= 4 \cdot$ ___   ___ = ___   Check: $\dfrac{}{16} = 4$ ___ = ___

9. $\dfrac{x}{2} = 32$ $\dfrac{x}{2} \cdot$ ___ $= 32 \cdot$ ___   ___ = ___   Check: $\dfrac{}{2} = 32$ ___ = ___

10. $\dfrac{y}{3} = 7$ $\dfrac{y}{3} \cdot$ ___ $= 7 \cdot$ ___   ___ = ___   Check: $\dfrac{}{3} = 7$ ___ = ___

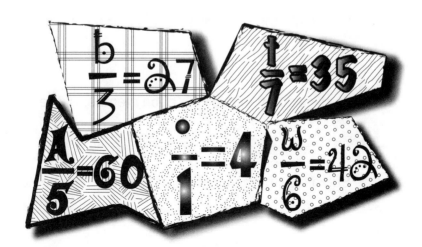

Name: _____ Date: _____

Ratios

Ratios may be written many ways. One way of writing a ratio is as a fraction. Examples of ratios written as fractions are $\frac{2}{5}$ and $\frac{10}{25}$ and $\frac{6}{30}$. To read the fraction $\frac{2}{5}$ as a ratio, you would read it as "two to five." This is the comparison form. The 2 is compared to 5. The ratio 2 to 5 can also be written as 2:5. We call this the colon form. You read it the same way you read the comparison form.

Directions: Write ratios for each of the following.

1. Write the ratio $\frac{3}{7}$ as a comparison.   _____ to _____

2. Write the ratio $\frac{2}{9}$ as a comparison.   _____ to _____

3. Write the ratio $\frac{5}{6}$ as a comparison.   _____ to _____

4. Write the ratio $\frac{4}{7}$ as a comparison.   _____ to _____

5. Write the ratio $\frac{8}{11}$ as a comparison.   _____ to _____

6. Write the ratio $\frac{2}{3}$ in the colon form.   _____ : _____

7. Write the ratio $\frac{2}{10}$ in the colon form.   _____ : _____

8. Write the ratio $\frac{1}{5}$ in the colon form.   _____ : _____

9. Write the ratio $\frac{12}{17}$ in the colon form.   _____ : _____

10. Write the ratio $\frac{9}{13}$ in the colon form.   _____ : _____

Write the ratio for each of the following.	Fraction	Comparison	Colon
11. The Wolves won 5 games and lost 12.	____	____ to ____	____ : ____
12. The soccer team won 7 games and lost 12.	____	____ to ____	____ : ____
13. The softball team won 10 games and lost 5.	____	____ to ____	____ : ____
14. The football team won 6 games and lost 4.	____	____ to ____	____ : ____
15. The baseball team won 9 games and lost 11.	____	____ to ____	____ : ____

Name: _____ Date: _____

Proportions

A proportion compares two equal ratios. Proportions may be written in fraction form. An example of a proportion is $\frac{3}{5} = \frac{6}{10}$. The comparison form is "3 is to 5 as 6 is to 10." The proportion is read "three is to five as six is to ten." Proportions may be written in the colon form as 3:5::6:10. It is read the same way.

The ratios in a proportion must be equal. In our example, $\frac{3}{5}$ and $\frac{6}{10}$ are equal. One way to check to see if your ratios are proportional is to check their cross products. The cross products must be equal.

$$\frac{3}{5} \diagdown\!\!\!\!\!\diagup \frac{6}{10}$$

$3 \cdot 10 = 30$ 3 and 10 are cross products
$5 \cdot 6 = 30$ 5 and 6 are cross products

Directions: Write each pair of ratios as a proportion and a cross product. The first one is done for you.

1. 2 is to 5   4 is to 10   proportion: __2__ : __5__ : : __4__ : __10__

   cross products: __2__ • __10__ as __5__ • __4__

2. 5 is to 3   10 is to 6   proportion: _____ : _____ : : _____ : _____

   cross products: _____ • _____ as _____ • _____

3. 1 is to 3   3 is to 9   proportion: _____ : _____ : : _____ : _____

   cross products: _____ • _____ as _____ • _____

4. 3 is to 5   9 is to 15   proportion: _____ : _____ : : _____ : _____

   cross products: _____ • _____ as _____ • _____

5. 2 is to 3   4 is to 6   proportion: _____ : _____ : : _____ : _____

   cross products: _____ • _____ as _____ • _____

6. 5 is to 7   10 is to 14   proportion: _____ : _____ : : _____ : _____

   cross products: _____ • _____ as _____ • _____

7. 3 is to 8   6 is to 16   proportion: _____ : _____ : : _____ : _____

   cross products: _____ • _____ as _____ • _____

8. 9 is to 1   27 is to 3   proportion: _____ : _____ : : _____ : _____

   cross products: _____ • _____ as _____ • _____

Name: _____ Date: _____

Cross Product Exercises

Directions: Solve the proportions for the unknown. The first one is done for you.

1. $\dfrac{2}{5} :: \dfrac{x}{10}$ $2 \cdot 10 = 20$ $20 = 5x$ $\dfrac{20}{5} = \dfrac{5x}{5}$ $x = 4$

$5 \cdot x = 5x$

2. $\dfrac{2}{3} :: \dfrac{x}{6}$ ___ • ___ = ___   ___ = ___ x ___ = ___ x $x =$ ___

___ • x = ___ x

3. $\dfrac{1}{4} :: \dfrac{x}{8}$ ___ • ___ = ___   ___ = ___ x ___ = ___ x $x =$ ___

___ • x = ___ x

4. $\dfrac{1}{3} :: \dfrac{x}{9}$ ___ • ___ = ___   ___ = ___ x ___ = ___ x $x =$ ___

___ • x = ___ x

5. $\dfrac{5}{6} :: \dfrac{x}{12}$ ___ • ___ = ___   ___ = ___ x ___ = ___ x $x =$ ___

___ • x = ___ x

6. $\dfrac{1}{9} :: \dfrac{x}{27}$ ___ • ___ = ___   ___ = ___ x ___ = ___ x $x =$ ___

___ • x = ___ x

24″ · 18″

12″ · x″

Name: _____ Date: _____

Finding the Mean

The mean, median, and mode are terms that measure the central tendency for a group of numbers. We use mean, median, and mode to help better understand the information a group of numbers is presenting. Each of the terms tells us something different for a group of numbers. Let's start with the mean.

> **Mean:** The mean is the average of a group of numbers. It is found by first finding the sum of a group of numbers. Then divide the sum by the total number of numbers.
>
> **Example:** $2 + 3 + 5 + 6 + 9 = 25$ 25 is the sum of five numbers. To find the average of the five numbers, divide 25 by 5.
>
> $25 \div 5 = 5$ The average of the five numbers is 5.

Directions: Find the mean for the following group of numbers.

14   12   16   20   16   14   18   40

Step 1: Arrange the numbers in order from smallest to largest.

Step 2: Find the sum:

_____ + _____ + _____ + _____ + _____ + _____ + _____ + _____ = _____

Step 3: Divide the sum by the number of numbers:

_____ ÷ _____ = _____

Step 4: Mean = _____

Directions: Find the mean for the following. Round to the nearest tenth if necessary.

1. 3, 2, 5, 3, 1, 3   sum = _____   mean = _____

2. 5, 8, 6, 2, 7, 9, 12   sum = _____   mean = _____

3. 11, 18, 12, 20, 12, 16, 17, 15   sum = _____   mean = _____

4. 77, 56, 34, 77, 45, 70   sum = _____   mean = _____

5. 31, 30, 31, 33, 36, 37, 31, 32   sum = _____   mean = _____

6. 108, 200, 253, 125, 200, 187   sum = _____   mean = _____

Name: _____ Date: _____

Finding the Mode

> **Mode:** The mode is the number in a group that occurs most often.
>
> ***Example:***   2, **3**, **3**, 5, 6, 9   In the group of numbers 2, 3, 3, 5, 6, and 9, the mode is the number 3.

Mode is useful because it can identify the most common event in a group. Let's say the scores on a test were 36, 68, 87, 87, 87, and 100. The mean for this set, 77.5, is below the scores of two-thirds of the test results. The mode, 87, can give us a better idea of how most of the class did on the test.

Directions: Find the mode for the following numbers.

14   12   16   20   16   14   18   40   16

Step 1:   Arrange the numbers in order from smallest to largest.

_____, _____, _____, _____, _____, _____, _____, _____, _____

Step 2:   The mode is the number that occurs most often.

Mode = _____

Directions: Find the mode for the following test scores.

1. 5, 8, 6, 2, 7, 9, 8   mode = _____

2. 11, 18, 12, 20, 12, 16, 17, 15   mode = _____

3. 77, 56, 34, 77, 45, 70   mode = _____

4. 31, 30, 31, 33, 36, 37, 31, 32   mode = _____

5. 108, 200, 253, 125, 200, 187   mode = _____

6. 11, 18, 12, 11, 18, 11, 20, 12, 18, 16, 17, 15, 11   mode = _____

Name: _____   Date: _____

Finding the Median

Median: The median is the number that is in the exact middle of a group of numbers.

> **Example:**   2, 3, **5**, 6, 9   In the group of numbers 2, 3, 5, 6, and 9, the median is the number 5.

If a group of numbers has an even number of numbers, there will be two numbers in the middle. Find the average of those two numbers, and that is the median.

> **Example:**   4, 5, 7, **8**, **9**, 12, 14, 16   8 and 9 are in the middle.
> Add 8 + 9 = 17   Divide 17 ÷ 2 = 8.5
> 8.5 is the median.

Knowing the median can help you understand what a group of numbers represents. In the test scores 48, 63, 85, 86, and 99, the median is 85. The median also tells us that two students scored below 85, and two students scored above 85.

Directions: Find the median for the following numbers.

30   20   38   42   24   27   35   45   40

Step 1: Arrange the numbers in order from smallest to largest.

_____, _____, _____, _____, _____, _____, _____, _____, _____

Step 2: Count from left and right until you get the number exactly in the middle of the group.

Step 3: The middle score is the median score. Median = _____

Directions: Find the median for the following test scores.

1. 5, 8, 6, 2, 7, 9, 12   median = _____

2. 77, 56, 34, 77, 45, 70, 57   median = _____

3. 31, 30, 31, 33, 36, 37, 31, 32, 33   median = _____

4. 108, 200, 253, 125, 200, 187, 156   median = _____

5. 7, 12, 5, 2, 3, 14, 4, 9   median = _____

6. 13, 8, 11, 26, 9, 5, 3, 6, 2, 10   median = _____

7. 25, 15, 23, 21, 32, 8, 7, 20, 18, 12, 4, 19   median = _____

Name: _____ Date: _____

Probability

You use probability every day. **Probability** tells us how likely, or unlikely, it is an event will occur. Probability is often written as a proper fraction. The numerator is the number of times an event occurs. The denominator is the number of possible events. When probability is written as a fraction, it is a ratio.

An **event** is one of the outcomes from the total number of events possible. A card is drawn from a deck of 52 cards. What is the probability that the card will be the king of hearts? The drawing of one card is an event. There are 52 different possible cards to draw for one event, and only one of them is the king of hearts. The probability of drawing the king of hearts is 1 event of 52 possibilities. The fractional ratio used to express this probability mathematically is $\frac{1}{52}$.

Similarly, the probability of drawing a card that is not the king of hearts can be expressed as $\frac{51}{52}$ because there are 51 cards you might draw that are not the king of hearts. Which one is more likely? The closer the numerator and denominator are, the more likely the event is to occur. Therefore, $\frac{51}{52}$ is more likely to occur than $\frac{1}{52}$. It's less likely you will draw the king of hearts than another card.

Directions: Decide which part of the fraction is the number of times an event occurs and which part is the total number of possible times an event could occur.

1. $\frac{1}{2}$ The number of events is _____. The number of possible events is _____.

2. $\frac{1}{5}$ The number of events is _____. The number of possible events is _____.

3. $\frac{1}{4}$ The number of events is _____. The number of possible events is _____.

4. $\frac{3}{10}$ The number of events is _____. The number of possible events is _____.

5. $\frac{2}{50}$ The number of events is _____. The number of possible events is _____.

6. $\frac{1}{100}$ The number of events is _____. The number of possible events is _____.

Probability Exercises

An outcome is one of the possibilities that may occur in an experiment. A bag contains 3 marbles. One marble is white. The drawing of one marble is an event. There are three possible outcomes, or events. What is the possibility that a marble drawn from the bag will be white?

1. The number of possible outcomes when a marble is drawn is _____.

2. The number of events in the single drawing is _____.

3. The ratio from the single drawing is **a)** $\frac{1}{2}$.　**b)** $\frac{1}{3}$.　**c)** $\frac{1}{5}$.

4. The probability that the drawn marble will be white is

   a) one of two.　　**b)** one of four.　　**c)** one of three.　　**d)** one of five.

5. The probability that the drawn marble will not be white is

   a) two of four.　　**b)** two of three.　　**c)** two of two.　　**d)** two of five.

Directions: Circle the correct answer for each of the following.

6. A coin is tossed one time. What is the probability that the coin will be heads?

   a) $\frac{1}{2}$　　**b)** $\frac{1}{3}$　　**c)** $\frac{1}{5}$　　**d)** $\frac{1}{4}$

7. A card is drawn from a deck of 52 cards. What is the probability the card will be a king?

   a) $\frac{1}{52}$　　**b)** $\frac{2}{52}$　　**c)** $\frac{3}{52}$　　**d)** $\frac{4}{52}$

8. A card is drawn from a deck of 52 cards. What is the probability the card will be a king or a queen?

   a) $\frac{2}{52}$　　**b)** $\frac{8}{52}$　　**c)** $\frac{10}{52}$　　**d)** $\frac{12}{52}$

9. A coin is tossed ten times. What is the number of possible events?

   a) 4　　**b)** 6　　**c)** 8　　**d)** 10

Name: _____ Date: _____

Probability Prediction

The probability of an event will be represented as a number between 0 and 1. A probability of 0 means the event will never occur. A probability of 1 means the event will always occur. Any fraction between 0 and 1 tells you how likely the event is to occur. The closer to 0, the less likely an event is. The closer to 1, the more likely an event is.

A die can be used to show the probability of an event between 0 and 1. The numbers on a die are 1, 2, 3, 4, 5, and 6. If the die is tossed, one of the numbers will always appear. That means the probability of a number not appearing is 0.

Directions: Circle the correct answer for each of the following.

1. When the die is tossed, the number of possible outcomes is

a) 3. **b)** 4. **c)** 5. **d)** 6.

2. The ratio that shows the probability that the number rolled will be the number 1 is

a) $\frac{1}{6}$. **b)** $\frac{2}{6}$. **c)** $\frac{3}{6}$. **d)** $\frac{4}{6}$.

3. The ratio that shows the probability that the number rolled will be the number 5 is

a) $\frac{1}{6}$. **b)** $\frac{2}{6}$. **c)** $\frac{3}{6}$. **d)** $\frac{4}{6}$.

4. The ratio that shows the probability that the number rolled will be any of the 6 numbers is

a) $\frac{1}{6}$. **b)** $\frac{3}{6}$. **c)** $\frac{5}{6}$. **d)** $\frac{6}{6}$.

A bag contains a black token, a white token, a green token, a red token, and a blue token.

5. The total number of possible events or outcomes for drawing a token from the bag is

a) 4. **b)** 5. **c)** 6. **d)** 7.

6. The probability that you will draw any one of the colored tokens on the first draw is

a) $\frac{2}{5}$. **b)** $\frac{3}{5}$. **c)** $\frac{4}{5}$. **d)** $\frac{5}{5}$

7. The probability that you will draw a green or blue token on the first draw is

a) $\frac{1}{5}$. **b)** $\frac{2}{5}$. **c)** $\frac{3}{5}$. **d)** $\frac{4}{5}$.

8. The probability that you will draw a green, white, or red token on the first draw is

a) $\frac{1}{5}$. **b)** $\frac{2}{5}$. **c)** $\frac{3}{5}$. **d)** $\frac{4}{5}$.

Name: _____ Date: _____

Learning About the Rectangular Coordinate System

Many people have become famous for their work in mathematics. René Descartes, a French mathematician of the seventeenth century, made an important contribution to mathematics. It was Descartes who developed the rectangular coordinate system.

A **rectangular coordinate system** is developed by drawing two perpendicular lines that are then numbered like a double number line from the point of origin.

The two perpendicular lines at right can be used to develop a rectangular system. The vertical line is called the **y-axis**, and the horizontal line is called the **x-axis**. The **origin**, or reference point, is zero.

The rectangular coordinate system can be used to locate points in a plane. Note that the x- and y-axes are numbered in equal units from the origin, or zero.

Rectangular Coordinate System A

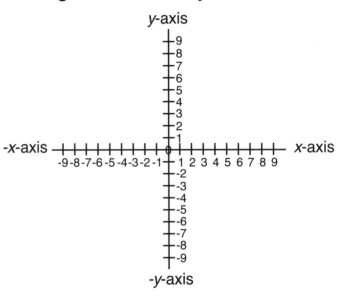

Directions: On Rectangular Coordinate System B below, complete the following.

Rectangular Coordinate System B

1. What number is located below the letter A? _____
   Which axis is the number on? _____
   Is the number positive or negative? _____

2. What number is located below the letter B? _____
   Which axis is the number on? _____
   Is the number positive or negative? _____

3. What number is located beside the letter C? _____
   Which axis is the number on? _____
   Is the number positive or negative? _____

4. What number is located beside the letter D? _____
   Which axis is the number on? _____
   Is the number positive or negative? _____

Name: _____ Date: _____

Learning About Coordinates

Rectangular Coordinate System C

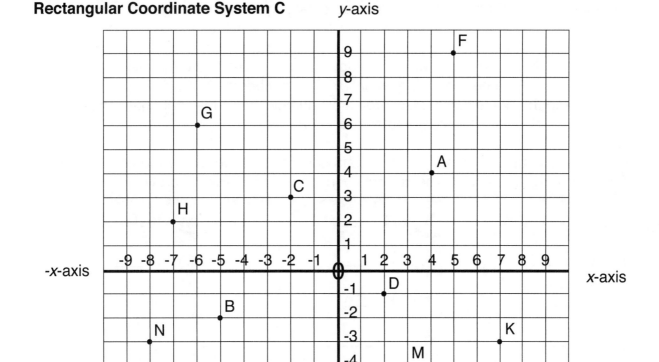

Rectangular Coordinate System C will help you understand how to locate coordinate points. A coordinate point is located by its distance from the origin on the *x*- and *y*-axes. Each point has two numbers locating it. The numbers are called the **coordinates**.

Let's locate point A.

Step 1: From the origin, count right on the *x*-axis to the number on the *x*-axis that is directly under the letter "A." The number is 4.

Step 2: From the origin, count up on the *y*-axis to the number that is on the same line as the letter "A." This number is also 4.

Step 3: These two numbers (4, 4) are called the coordinates for locating point A.

The coordinate (number) for the *x*-axis is always written first. Thus, (4, 4) means +4 on the *x*-axis and +4 on the *y*-axis.

Name: _____ Date: _____

Learning About Coordinates *(continued)*

Let's locate point B using Rectangular Coordinate System C on page 61.

Step 1: From the origin, count left on the *x*-axis to the number on the *x*-axis that is directly above the letter "B." The number is -5.

Step 2: From the origin, count down on the *y*-axis to the number that is on the same line as the letter "B." The number is -2.

Step 3: Write these two coordinates (numbers) with the coordinate on the *x*-axis first. The coordinates are -5, -2.

Directions: Use Rectangular Coordinate System C on page 61 to locate the coordinates for each of the following points. Write the correct coordinates in the spaces provided.

1. C _____, _____

2. D _____, _____

3. E _____, _____

4. F _____, _____

5. G _____, _____

6. H _____, _____

7. I _____, _____

8. J _____, _____

9. K _____, _____

10. L _____, _____

11. M _____, _____

12. N _____, _____

Directions: Answer the following about the coordinates above.

13. For B, which number is the *x*-coordinate? _____

14. For C, which number is the *y*-coordinate? _____

15. For D, which number is the *y*-coordinate? _____

16. For E, which number is the *x*-coordinate? _____

17. For F, which number is the *y*-coordinate? _____

18. For G, which number is the *x*-coordinate? _____

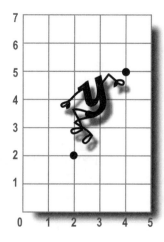

Directions: Circle the coordinate indicated in each of the following. The first one is done for you.

19. ③, 4   (the *x*-coordinate)

20. -2, 5   (the *y*-coordinate)

21. -7, -6 (the *y*-coordinate)

22. 8, -3   (the *y*-coordinate)

23. -3, 4   (the *x*-coordinate)

24. -9, -3 (the *x*-coordinate)

Name: _____ Date: _____

Plotting the Point

For each set of coordinates there is exactly one point located on the rectangular coordinate system. Locating a point on the rectangular coordinate system is called **plotting the point**.

Directions: Use Rectangular Coordinate System D to plot the points below. Place a dot (•) on the graph to locate each point. Then place the letter representing that point next to each dot.

Rectangular Coordinate System D

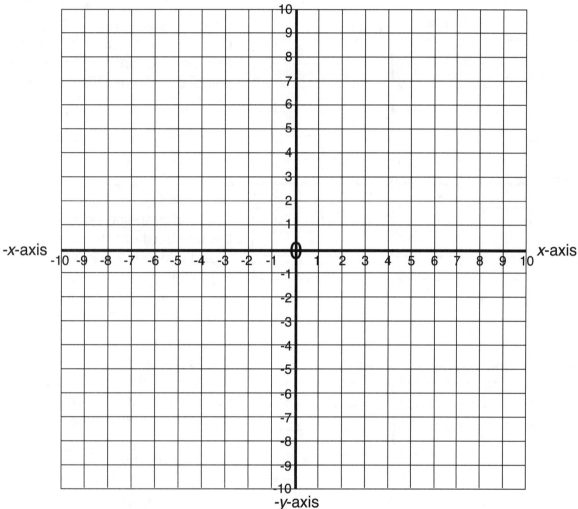

Plot the point for each set of coordinates.

A. 3, 3	**E.** 1, 8	**I.** 6, -5	**M.** 0, -5
B. -4, -5	**F.** 8, 1	**J.** 4, -3	**N.** -5, 0
C. -4, -2	**G.** -1, -4	**K.** -5, 5	**O.** 0, 0
D. 5, 7	**H.** -5, 3	**L.** 1, 1	**P.** 7, -7

Name: _____ Date: _____

The Rectangular Coordinate System and Equations

The rectangular coordinate system is used to graph equations. When an equation is graphed, the results are visual. Graphing an equation is useful in finding the solutions (answers) to equations.

Learning to Graph Equations

In using the rectangular coordinate system to graph equations, the exact location of coordinates and accurately drawing lines to connect the coordinate points are important. The following exercises will develop the skills of locating coordinates and connecting the located points.

Rectangular Coordinate System E

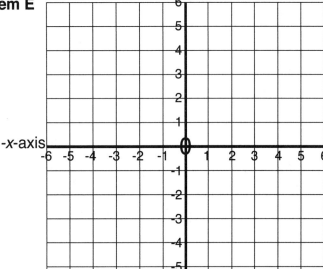

Directions: Using Rectangular Coordinate System E, locate the following coordinates and connect each pair of coordinates with a straight line.

1. 2, 4; -3, -4
2. 4, 3; -1, -3
3. -3, 5; 4, -2
4. 3, 5; -4, -2

In graphing equations, locating the points where the line crosses the x- and y-axes is key in finding solutions to problems.

In **4.** above, the line crosses the x-axis at -2, 0 and the y-axis at 0, 2.

Directions: Draw lines connecting the following points on Rectangular Coordinate System F, and write the coordinates locating where the lines cross the x- and y-axes.

Rectangular Coordinate System F

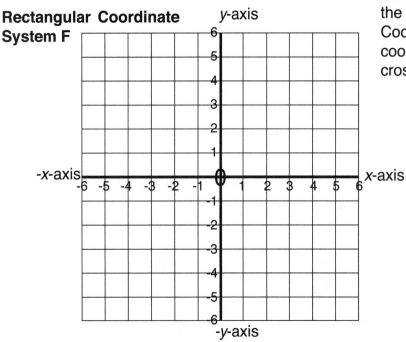

1. 3, 4; -4, -3
   Crosses the x-axis at ____, ____
   Crosses the y-axis at ____, ____

2. -1, 6; 6, -1
   Crosses the x-axis at ____, ____
   Crosses the y-axis at ____, ____

3. 6, 3; 2, -3
   Crosses the x-axis at ____, ____
   Crosses the y-axis at ____, ____

Name: _____ Date: _____

Linear Equations With Two Variables

You have learned that variables are the letters used in equations to represent numbers. The equation $x = y + 3$ can be used to demonstrate how variables are used in equations.

$x = y + 3$	If $x = 7$, then y must equal 4. If $x = 10$, then y must equal 7. If $x = 40$, then y must equal 37. If $x = -4$, then y must equal -7.

In $x = y + 3$, the value of y depends on the value assigned to x. The variable is y, since it may have different values.

The equation $x = y + 3$ is a linear equation. **A linear equation will be a straight line when graphed on a rectangular coordinate system.**

Many linear equations will be in a form like $2x + y = 16$.

$2x + y = 16$	If $x = 4$, then y equals 8. If $x = 3$, then y equals 10. If $x = 7$, then y equals 2.

Directions: Solve the following (use the values for the variables indicated to solve each equation).

1. $x + y = 12$ What does y equal if $x =$ 3? _____   4? _____   9? _____

2. $2x + y = 20$ What does y equal if $x =$ 7? _____   5? _____   8? _____

3. $7 + x = y$ What does y equal if $x =$ 12? _____   10? _____   1? _____

4. $5x + y = 30$ What does y equal if $x =$ 10? _____   8? _____   7? _____

5. $3x + 2y = 12$ What does y equal if $x =$ 2? _____   1? _____   0? _____

6. $7 + 2y = x$ What does y equal if $x =$ 9? _____   11? _____   23? _____

7. $6x - 2 = y$ What does y equal if $x =$ 1? _____   3? _____   -2? _____

8. $4x - 3 = y$ What does y equal if $x =$ -1? _____   -2? _____   -3? _____

Name: _____ Date: _____

Plotting Points for Linear Equations

When plotting points for a linear equation on a rectangular coordinate system, a table of values should be developed. In making a table of values, you are finding the values that *x* and *y* might represent. A table of values for *x* = *y* + 2 is at the right.

	x	y	x = y + 2
1.	5	3	→ 5 = 3 + 2
2.	4	2	→ 4 = 2 + 2
3.	3	1	→ 3 = 1 + 2
4.	-5	-7	→ -5 = -7 + 2
5.	2	0	→ 2 = 0 + 2
6.	-1	-3	→ -1 = -3 + 2

Directions: The *x* and *y* values become the coordinates for plotting the points on the rectangular coordinate system. Use the table above and write the coordinates for each point.

1. ____ , ____   2. ____ , ____   3. ____ , ____

4. ____ , ____   5. ____ , ____   6. ____ , ____

Directions: Plot the coordinates for the six points above on Rectangular Coordinate System G.

Rectangular Coordinate System G

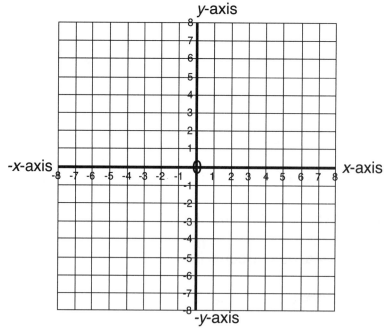

Directions: Complete the following.

7. Draw a line connecting the points plotted on Rectangular Coordinate System G.

8. Write the coordinates locating where the line crosses the *x*-axis.   ____ , ____

9. Write the coordinates locating where the line crosses the *y*-axis.   ____ , ____

10. The line drawn on Rectangular Coordinate System G represents the linear equation

    x = ____ + ____ .

Name: _____ Date: _____

 ## Plotting Points for Linear Equations *(continued)*

Directions: Make a table of values for the following linear equations. Plot the coordinate points on Rectangular Coordinate System H. Then draw a line connecting the plotted points for each equation.

11. $y = 2x$

x	y
____ = 2 ____	
____ = 2 ____	
____ = 2 ____	
____ = 2 ____	

12. $2x + y = 8$

x	y
2 ____ + ____ = 8	
2 ____ + ____ = 8	
2 ____ + ____ = 8	
2 ____ + ____ = 8	

13. $3x + 1 = y$

x	y
3 ____ + 1 = ____	
3 ____ + 1 = ____	
3 ____ + 1 = ____	
3 ____ + 1 = ____	

Rectangular Coordinate System H

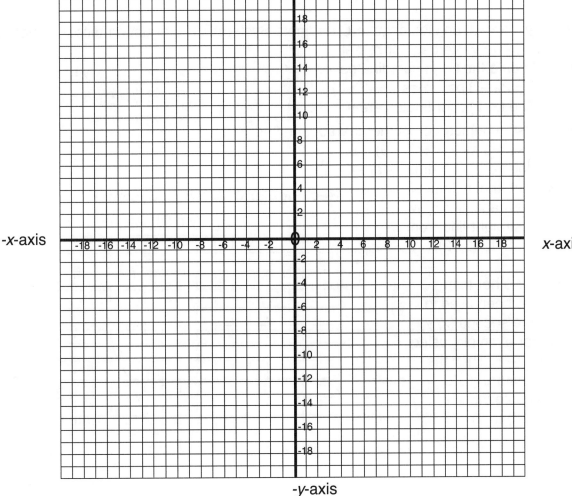

Name: _____ Date: _____

Finding the Slope and *y*-Intercept of a Straight Line

Finding the slope of a linear equation and where the line **intercepts** (crosses) the *y*-axis are important in the study of algebra.

To find the slope and *y*-intercept of a linear equation, the equation must be written in the form $y = mx + b$.

The equation $2x - y = 8$ is not in the slope-intercept form. A linear equation is in the **slope-intercept form** when the equation is rewritten with *y* as one member of the equation.

$2x - y = 8$	Rewrite $2x - y = 8$ with *y* as one member of the equation.
$2x - y + y = 8 + y$	Add $+y$ to each member of the equation.
$2x = 8 + y$	
$2x - 8 = 8 - 8 + y$	Subtract 8 from each member of the equation.
$2x - 8 = y$	Rewrite the equation with *y* as the left member.
$y = 2x - 8$	The equation is now in the form $y = mx + b$.

Graph $y = 2x - 8$ on Rectangular Coordinate System I. The equation tells you that the slope, or *m*, is 2. The *y*-intercept, or *b*, is -8.

Step 1: Locate the (*x*, *y*) coordinates for $x = 0$.
$y = 2x - 8$ becomes $y = (2 \cdot 0) - 8$
The (*x*, *y*) coordinates are (0, -8).

Step 2: Use a number for *x* other than 0, and find *y*.
Using 3 for *x*, $y = (2 \cdot 3) - 8$. $y = -2$
The (*x*, *y*) coordinates are (3, -2).

x	y		$y = 2x - 8$
0	-8	→	$-8 = (2 \cdot 0) - 8$
3	-2	→	$-2 = (2 \cdot 3) - 8$

Step 3: Plot the points on the graph, and draw a straight line from (0,-8) to (3, -2).

A number other than $x = 3$ could have been used in Step 2 to find the second (*x*, *y*) coordinates. For example, using $x = 5$, $y = (2 \cdot 5) - 8$. Then the (*x*, *y*) coordinates are (5, 2). A straight line could then be drawn from (0, -8) to (5, 2).

Rectangular Coordinate System I

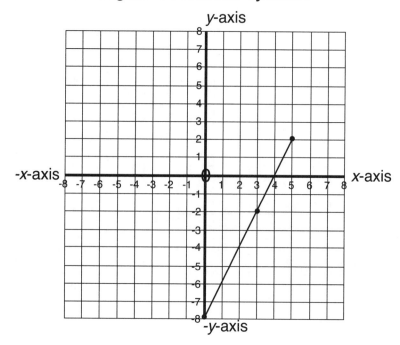

Name: _____ Date: _____

Finding the Slope and *y*-Intercept
of a Straight Line *(continued)*

Determining the Slope and *y*-Intercept of $y = 2x - 8$.

The equation $y = 2x - 8$ is in the slope-intercept form $y = mx + b$.

Directions: Answer the following.

1. In the equation $y = mx + b$, the letter *m* is the coefficient of *x*. In the equation $y = 2x - 8$, the coefficient of *x* is the number _____.

2. In the equation $y = mx + b$, the letter *b* locates the point where the graph crosses the *y*-axis. In the equation $y = 2x - 8$, the number _____ replaces the letter *b* in the equation $y = mx + b$.

3. The line drawn to represent the linear equation $y = 2x - 8$ crosses the *y*-axis at the point _____.

Remember, the slope and *y*-intercept of a line are found using the following steps.

Step 1. Rewrite the equation so *y* is a member by itself on one side of the equation.

Step 2. The coefficient for *x* is the slope of the line.

Step 3. The constant term *b* must be located using the coordinates $(0, b)$ on the *y*-axis. This is the point where the line intercepts (crosses) the *y*-axis.

Step 4. Use a number for *x* other than 0 in the equation to find a second set of (x, y) coordinates.

Step 5. Plot the points on the graph, and draw a straight line from $(0, b)$ to the second set of (x, y) coordinates.

Directions: Rewrite the following equations in the slope-intercept form $y = mx + b$.

4. $2y = 4x + 8$ Divide each side of the equation by 2, leaving *y* on one side.

   $y =$ ____$x +$ ____

5. $4y = 8x + 4$ Divide each side of the equation by 4, leaving *y* on one side.

   $y =$ ____$x +$ ____

6. $2y = x - 6$ Divide each side of the equation by 2, leaving *y* on one side.

   $y =$ ____$x -$ ____

Directions: Find the *y*-intercept (the 0, *b* coordinate) for $y = mx + b$ in each of the following equations. Write as (x, y) coordinates.

7. $y = 2x + 4$ _____

8. $y = 2x + 1$ _____

9. $y = \frac{1}{2}x - 3$ _____

Answer Key

Number Systems (p. 1)
1. 1   **2.** 0   **3.** 0   **4.** negative
5. negative or minus   **6.** positive or plus
7. -4   **8.** +7   **9.** -60

The Integer Number System (p. 3)
1. +13   **2.** +2   **3.** -1   **4.** -4
5. +6   **6.** -6   **7.** -12
8. 5   **9.** 6, negative   **10.** 7, negative
11. 8, positive   **12.** negative   **13.** positive
14. -2   **15.** +40   **16.** -800   **17.** -6
18. +249   **19.** -2,101   **20.** +5,732

Number Properties (p. 4)
1. 10, 3   **2.** 10, 25   **3.** 360, 210
4. 20, 20   **5.** 65, 25
7. 35 + 64 = 64 + 35
8. 111 + 742 = 742 + 111
9. 37 + 94 = 94 + 37
10. 2,101 + 642 = 642 + 2,101
11. 10 + 18 = 18 + 10
12. 12 + 23 = 23 + 12

Whole Numbers (p. 5)
Teacher check number line.
1. 11   **2.** 11   **3.** 11   **4.** 11
5. 13   **6.** 13   **7.** 11   **8.** 11
9. 14   **10.** 14   **11.** sum

Commutative Property for Multiplication (p. 6)
1. 12   **2.** 12   **3.** 10   **4.** 10
5. 21   **6.** 21   **7.** 20   **8.** 20
9. 5 • 4 = 4 • 5
10. 12 • 6 = 6 • 12
11. 111 • 246 = 246 • 111
12. 1,074 • 917 = 917 • 1,074
13. 47 • 86 = 86 • 47
14. 3,440   **15.** 3,440   **16.** 616,000
17. 616,000   **18. and 19.** Answers will vary.
20. The answer to the second question is the same as the answer to the first. The order of the numbers multiplied does not change the product, so by rearranging the order, you can just write down the zeroes and continue with the rest of the problem.

Associative Property for Addition (p. 7)
1. 8 + 7 = 15   **2.** 13 + 2 = 15
3. 10 + 5 = 15   **4.** 9 + 7 = 16
5. 15 + 1 = 16   **6.** 10 + 6 = 16
7. 15 + 5 = 20   **8.** 12 + 8 = 20
9. 17 + 3 = 20   **10.** 10 + 13 = 23
11. 16 + 7 = 23   **12.** 17 + 6 = 23
The order of the numbers may vary. Possible order includes:
13. (9 + 1) + (8 + 4) = 22
14. (12 + 8) + (4 + 1) = 25
15. (14 + 6) + (3 + 9) = 32
16. (18 + 7) + (10 + 7) = 42
17. (25 + 5) + (16 + 4) = 50
18. (29 + 10) + (16 + 4) = 59
19. (61 + 9) + (14 + 6) = 90
20. (13 + 7) + (6 + 11) = 37

Associative Property for Multiplication (p. 8)
1. 18 • 4 = 72   **2.** 6 • 12 = 72
3. 3 • 24 = 72   **4.** 36 • 5 = 180
5. 9 • 20 = 180   **6.** 45 • 4 = 180
7. 24 • 6 = 144   **8.** 12 • 12 = 144
9. 72 • 2 = 144   **10.** 45 • 5 = 225
11. 15 • 15 = 225   **12.** 3 • 75 = 225
The order of the numbers may vary. Possible order includes:
13. (15 • 3) • (6 • 5) = 45 • 30 = 1,350
14. (5 • 2) • (12 • 8) = 10 • 96 = 960
15. (8 • 3) • (5 • 2) = 24 • 10 = 240
16. (14 • 8) • (5 • 4) = 112 • 20 = 2,240
17. (17 • 2) • (8 • 5) = 34 • 40 = 1,360
18. (3 • 24) • (5 • 2) = 72 • 10 = 720
19. (25 • 4) • (5 • 2) = 100 • 10 = 1,000
20. (3 • 6) • (10 • 11) = 18 • 110 = 1,980

Distributive Property of Multiplication Over Addition (p. 9)
1. 30 + 6, 6, 150 + 30 = 180
2. 40 + 2, 40, 2, 360 + 18 = 378
3. 80 + 8, 80, 8, 960 + 96 = 1,056
4. 30 + 5, 30, 5, 210 + 35 = 245
5. 70 + 8, 70, 8, 420 + 48 = 468
6. 40 + 8, 40, 8, 320 + 64 = 384
7. 200 + 68, 200, 68, 2,800 + 952 = 3,752
8. 100 + 60, 100, 60, 1,800 + 1,080 = 2,880
9. 30 + 8, 30, 8, 90 + 24 = 114
10. 70 + 9, 70, 9, 770 + 99 = 869

Properties of Subtraction and Division (p. 10)
1. =   2. =   3. =   4. ≠
5. ≠   6. ≠   7. ≠

Properties of Zero/Identity Elements (p. 11)
1. number   2. zero   3. one
4. A   5. B   6. C   7. A   8. B
9. B   10. B   11. B   12. C

Order of Operations (p. 12)
1. $20 + 6 = 26$ 2. $54 + 24 = 78$
3. $32 + 14 = 46$ 4. $18 + 12 = 30$
5. $20 - 6 = 14$ 6. $54 - 24 = 30$
7. $32 - 14 = 18$ 8. $18 - 12 = 6$
9. 24, $24 + 4 = 28$ 10. 2, $2 + 32, 34, 28$
11. 24, $24 - 4 = 31 - 4 = 27$
12. 30, $30 - 2, 28, 32$ 13. 20, $20 + 4, 24, 20$

Addition of Integers (p. 13)
1. +11   2. -8   3. -4   4. +3
5. -6   6. -10   7. +8   8. +7

Addition of Integers: Exercises (p. 14)
Rule 1: When adding two integers with the same sign, add the numbers and place the sign of the numbers before the answer.

Rule 2: When adding two numbers with unlike signs, first find the difference between the two numbers. Then place the sign of the larger number before the answer.

1. +10   2. -7   3. +6   4. -5
5. +3   6. -261   7. +68   8. +101
9. -15   10. -65   11. -2   12. +17
13. +114   14. +95   15. -38   16. -58
17. +80   18. -123   19. -476   20. -71
21. +35   22. +297   23. -776   24. +152
25. -103

Subtraction of Integers: Rule/Exercises (p. 16)
1. -10, -10   2. -3, -3   3. -5, -5
4. +5, +5   5. +4, +4   6. +20, +20
7. -1, -1

Addition and Subtraction of Integers: Exercises (p. 17)
1. +8   2. +14   3. -11   4. -19
5. -3   6. +7   7. -4   8. +5
9. -76   10. -47   11. +23   12. -30
13. +3   14. -8   15. +1   16. -4
17. -9   18. -324

Multiplication of Integers (p. 18)
1. Rule 1   2. Rule 1   3. Rule 2   4. Rule 2
5. 8   6. -21   7. 30   8. 48
9. 72   10. 72   11. -40   12. 36
13. 88   14. -49   15. -25   16. -42
17. -144   18. 36   19. -286   20. 180

Division of Integers (p. 19)
1. 4   2. 5   3. -4   4. 8
5. -6   6. -16   7. -4   8. 4
9. -4   10. -15   11. -5   12. 9
13. 4   14. 4   15. 7   16. 6
17. 7   18. -27   19. -7   20. 11

Variables (p. 20)
Answers will vary according to the number chosen for each variable. Variables and constants are:
1. x, 5   2. y, 6   3. m, 9   4. t, 17
5. p, 25

Variables and Multiplication (p. 21)
1. 2, 3, a 2. 7, 4, a 3. 5, 9, n
4. 8, 7, b 5. 4, 12, p 6. 12, 10, x
7. 6, 15, x 8. 5, 20, y 9. 3, 14, t
10. 9, 8, w

Variables and Division/Variable Exercises (p. 22)
1. 7, 14, b 2. 4, 20, t 3. 3, 18, s
4. 6, 24, y 5. 9, 36, y 6. 3, 72, m
7. 11, 88, m 8. 7, 49, x 9. 14
10. 3   11. 4   12. 22   13. 4
14. 4   15. 21   16. 7   17. 18
18. 8   19. 9   20. 60

Exponents (p. 23)
1. base, exponent   2. base, exponent
3. exponent, base   4. base, exponent
5. exponent, base   6. multiplied
7. 4   8. $3 \cdot 3 = 9$ 9. $2 \cdot 2 \cdot 2 = 8$
10. $4 \cdot 4 \cdot 4 = 64$ 11. $5 \cdot 5 = 25$
12. $10 \cdot 10 \cdot 10 = 1,000$ 13. $8 \cdot 8 \cdot 8 = 512$
14. $12 \cdot 12 = 144$
15. $5 \cdot 5 \cdot 5 \cdot 5 = 625$

Exponents: Maximum Power, Minimum Space (p. 24)
1. ^{2} 2. ^{3} 3. ^{2} 4. ^{4} 5. 9
6. 7   7. 2   8. 5^0 9. 2^1 10. 7^0

Exponents: Rules to Remember (p. 25)

1. 7   **2.** 1   **3.** 10   **4.** 4
5. 0   **6.** 0   **7.** 0   **8.** 1
9. 4   **10.** 27   **11.** 4   **12.** 25
13. -8   **14.** 16   **15.** 343   **16.** -64
17. -125   **18.** 100   **19.** -1,000   **20.** -1,024

Adding and Subtracting Exponents (p. 26)

2. $2+3 = 2^5 = 2 \cdot 2 \cdot 2 \cdot 2 \cdot 2 = 32$
3. $5^{2+4} = 5^6 = 5 \cdot 5 \cdot 5 \cdot 5 \cdot 5 \cdot 5 = 15{,}625$
4. $6^{1+2} = 6^3 = 6 \cdot 6 \cdot 6 = 216$
5. $2^{1+1} = 2^2 = 2 \cdot 2 = 4$
6. $10^{1+1} = 10^2 = 10 \cdot 10 = 100$
7. $7^{2+1} = 7^3 = 7 \cdot 7 \cdot 7 = 343$
8. $4^{2+0} = 4^2 = 4 \cdot 4 = 16$
9. $5^{0+1} = 5^1 = 5$
11. 4^{-2}
12. $\dfrac{2^5}{2^4} = 2^{5-4} = 2^1$ **13.** $\dfrac{7^4}{7^6} = 7^{4-6} = 7^{-2}$
14. $\dfrac{6^5}{6^9} = 6^{5-9} = 6^{-4}$ **15.** $\dfrac{9^3}{9^1} = 9^{3-1} = 9^2$

Multiplying Exponents (p. 27)

2. $3 \cdot 2,\ ^6,\ 64$ **3.** $2 \cdot 2 = 3^4 = 81$
4. $5^{2 \cdot 2} = 5^4 = 625$ **5.** $4^{2 \cdot 2} = 4^4 = 256$
6. $3^{1 \cdot 2} = 3^2 = 9$ **7.** $6^{0 \cdot 2} = 6^0 = 1$
8. $2^{3 \cdot 3} = 2^9 = 512$ **9.** $3^{3 \cdot 2} = 3^6 = 729$
10. $2^{2 \cdot 3} = 2^6 = 64$ **11.** $4^{1 \cdot 2} = 4^2 = 16$
12. $10^{2 \cdot 2} = 10^4 = 10{,}000$

Zero and Negative Integer Exponents (p. 28)

1. 1   **2.** 5^2, 25   **3.** $\frac{1}{33}$, $\frac{1}{27}$ **4.** 1
5. $\frac{1}{100}$ **6.** $\frac{1}{100}$ **7.** 1   **8.** 4
9. $\frac{1}{49}$ **10.** 100   **11.** 16   **12.** 1
13. 64   **14.** 1,000   **15.** 1   **16.** $\frac{1}{8}$
17. $\frac{1}{25}$ **18.** $\frac{1}{16}$ **19.** $\frac{1}{9}$ **20.** 6
21. 125   **22.** 47   **23.** 35   **24.** 17
25. 3   **26.** 6   **27.** 145   **28.** $3\frac{3}{4}$
29. $\frac{35}{72}$ **30.** -72

Scientific Notation (p. 29)

2. $20 \cdot 1{,}000{,}000 = 20 \cdot 10^6$
3. $48 \cdot 1{,}000{,}000 = 48 \cdot 10^6$
4. $72 \cdot 1{,}000{,}000 = 72 \cdot 10^6$
5. $97 \cdot 1{,}000{,}000 = 97 \cdot 10^6$
6. $26 \cdot 1{,}000 = 26 \cdot 10^3$
7. $58 \cdot 1{,}000 = 58 \cdot 10^3$
8. $2 \cdot 1{,}000 = 2 \cdot 10^3$
9. $3 \cdot 100 = 3 \cdot 10^2$
10. $20 \cdot 1{,}000 = 20 \cdot 10^3$

Simplifying Large Numbers With Scientific Notation (p. 30)

1. 10^7, 10,000,000
2. $4.8 \cdot 10^7 = 4.8 \cdot 10{,}000{,}000$
3. $2.6 \cdot 10^7 = 2.6 \cdot 10{,}000{,}000$
4. $10^3 = 3.6 \cdot 1{,}000$
5. $3.6 \cdot 10^4 = 3.6 \cdot 10{,}000$
6. $10^3 = 5.5 \cdot 1{,}000$
7. $5.5 \cdot 10^4 = 5.5 \cdot 10{,}000$
8. $5.5 \cdot 10^7 = 5.5 \cdot 10{,}000{,}000$
9. $10^9 = 2.78 \cdot 1{,}000{,}000{,}000$
10. $6.09 \cdot 10^{11} = 6.09 \cdot 100{,}000{,}000{,}000$

Learning About Factoring (p. 31)

1. 1, 2, 4, 8   **2.** 1, 3, 9
3. 1, 2, 4, 8, 16   **4.** 1, 3, 5, 15

Learning About Prime Factors (p. 32)

1. 2, 2, 3   **2.** 2, 2, 2, 3
3. 2, 2, 2, 2, 2   **4.** 2, 2, 2, 2, 3
5. 2, 2, 2, 2, 2, 3   **6.** 2, 2, 2, 11
7. 2, 2, 59   **8.** 2, 2, 2, 2, 2, 2, 2, 2, 2

Finding Prime Factors (p. 33)

1. 2, 7   **2.** 2, 2, 13
3. 2, 3, 3, 5   **4.** 2, 3, 3, 7
5. 2, 3, 3, 19   **6.** 2, 2, 107
7. $2 \cdot 7$ **8.** $2 \cdot 2 \cdot 13 = 52$
9. $2 \cdot 3 \cdot 3 \cdot 5$ **10.** $2 \cdot 3 \cdot 3 \cdot 7 = 126$
11. $2 \cdot 3 \cdot 3 \cdot 19 = 342$ **12.** $2 \cdot 2 \cdot 107 = 428$
Teacher check factor trees.

Finding the Greatest Common Factor (p. 35)

1. prime for 12: 2, 2, 3
     prime for 18: 2, 3, 3   GCF: $2 \cdot 3 = 6$
2. prime for 24: 2, 2, 2, 3
     prime for 12: 2, 2, 3   GCF: $2 \cdot 2 \cdot 3 = 12$
3. prime for 36: 2, 2, 3, 3
     prime for 54: 2, 3, 3, 3   GCF: $2 \cdot 3 \cdot 3 = 18$
4. prime for 18: 2, 3, 3
     prime for 30: 2, 3, 5   GCF: $2 \cdot 3 = 6$
5. prime for 18: 2, 3, 3
     prime for 27: 3, 3, 3   GCF: $3 \cdot 3 = 9$
6. prime for 56: 2, 2, 2, 7
     prime for 16: 2, 2, 2, 2   GCF: $2 \cdot 2 \cdot 2 = 8$
7. prime for 93: 3, 31
     prime for 69: 3, 23   GCF: 3
8. prime for 72: 2, 2, 2, 3, 3
     prime for 216: 2, 2, 2, 3, 3, 3
     GCF: $2 \cdot 2 \cdot 2 \cdot 3 \cdot 3 = 72$

Learning About the Least Common Multiple (p. 36)
1. 10, 15, 20, 25, 30, 35
   14, 21, 28, 35, 42, 49   LCM = 35
2. 12, 18, 24, 30, 36
   20, 30, 40, 50, 60   LCM = 30
3. 20   4. 42   5. 90   6. 75
7. 180   8. 42   9. 136   10. 132

Radicals and Roots (p. 37)
1. $\sqrt{}$ 2. radicand
3. square root of four   4. cube root of eight
5. fourth root of sixteen

Finding Square Roots (p. 38)
1. 2   2. 3   3. 4   4. 6   5. 7
6. 8   7. 10   8. 5   9. 9   10. 12
11. 2   12. 6   13. 10   14. 7
15. $\sqrt{9}$ 16. $\sqrt{64}$ 17. $\sqrt{81}$
18. $\sqrt{25}$ 19. $\sqrt{144}$ 20. $\sqrt{16}$

Adding Radicals (p. 39)
1. 10   2. (4 + 3), 7   3. (2 + 4 + 3), 9
4. $(10 + 8 + 2)\sqrt{3} = 20\sqrt{3}$
5. $(9 + 5)\sqrt{5} = 14\sqrt{5}$ 6. $23\sqrt{29}$
7. $25\sqrt{31}$ 8. (1 + 2), 3
9. (3 + 19 + 1), 23   10. $13\sqrt{7}$

Subtracting Radicals (p. 40)
1. 3, 5
2. $(14 - 7)\sqrt{11} = 7\sqrt{11}$
3. $(32 - 15)\sqrt{7} = 17\sqrt{7}$
4. $(5 - 2 - 1)\sqrt{31} = 2\sqrt{31}$
5. $(8 - 10)\sqrt{15} = -2\sqrt{15}$
6. $(7 - 11)\sqrt{3} = -4\sqrt{3}$
7. $(26 - 5 - 23)\sqrt{8} = -2\sqrt{8}$
8. $\sqrt{6}$
9. $5\sqrt{41}$
10. $(10 + 8 - 5)\sqrt{3} = 13\sqrt{3}$
11. $(27 - 13 + 2 - 8)\sqrt{5} = 8\sqrt{5}$
12. $(14 - 18 + 2)\sqrt{11} = -2\sqrt{11}$

Multiplying and Dividing Radicals (p. 41)
1. $\sqrt{9}$, 3   2. $\sqrt[4]{16}$, 2   3. $\sqrt{16}$, 4
4. $\sqrt{4}$, 2   5. $\sqrt{49}$, 7   6. $\sqrt{64}$, 8
7. $\sqrt[3]{27}$, 3   8. $\sqrt{36}$, 6   9. $\sqrt{25}$, 5
10. $\sqrt{100}$, 10   11. 2   12. 2
13. $\sqrt{9}$, 3   14. $\sqrt{25}$, 5   15. $\sqrt[5]{32}$, 2
16. $\sqrt{25}$, 5   17. $\sqrt[3]{27}$, 3   18. $\sqrt{4}$, 2
19. $\sqrt[4]{625}$, 5   20. $\sqrt{4}$, 2

Simplifying Radicals (p. 42)
1. $\sqrt{4 \cdot 3}$, $\sqrt{3}$, $\sqrt{3}$, $\sqrt{3}$
2. $\sqrt{9 \cdot 2}$, $\sqrt{2}$, $\sqrt{2}$, $3\sqrt{2}$
3. $\sqrt{4 \cdot 5}$, $\sqrt{4}$, $\sqrt{5}$, $2 \cdot \sqrt{5}$, $2\sqrt{5}$
4. $\sqrt{9 \cdot 3}$, $\sqrt{9}$, $\sqrt{3}$, $3 \cdot \sqrt{3}$, $3\sqrt{3}$
5. $\sqrt{4 \cdot 2}$, $\sqrt{4}$, $\sqrt{2}$, $2 \cdot \sqrt{2}$, $2\sqrt{2}$
6. $\sqrt{4 \cdot 6}$, $\sqrt{4}$, $\sqrt{6}$, $2 \cdot \sqrt{6}$, $2\sqrt{6}$
7. $\sqrt{4 \cdot 8}$, $\sqrt{4} \cdot \sqrt{8}$, $2 \cdot \sqrt{8}$, $2\sqrt{8}$
8. $\sqrt{25 \cdot 2}$, $\sqrt{25} \cdot \sqrt{2}$, $5 \cdot \sqrt{2}$, $5\sqrt{2}$
9. $\sqrt{16 \cdot 3}$, $\sqrt{16} \cdot \sqrt{3}$, $4 \cdot \sqrt{3}$, $4\sqrt{3}$
10. $\sqrt{9 \cdot 5}$, $\sqrt{9} \cdot \sqrt{5}$, $3 \cdot \sqrt{5}$, $3\sqrt{5}$
11. 4   12. 7   13. 6   14. 5
15. 3   16. 10   17. 12   18. 8

Multiplying and Simplifying Radicals (p. 43)
1. $\sqrt{45} = \sqrt{9} = 3 \cdot \sqrt{5} = 3\sqrt{5}$
2. $\sqrt{12} = \sqrt{4} = 2 \cdot \sqrt{3} = 2\sqrt{3}$
3. $\sqrt{18} = \sqrt{9} \cdot \sqrt{2} = 3 \cdot \sqrt{2} = 3\sqrt{2}$
4. $\sqrt{24} = \sqrt{4} \cdot \sqrt{6} = 2 \cdot \sqrt{6} = 2\sqrt{6}$
5. $\sqrt{28} = \sqrt{4} \cdot \sqrt{7} = 2 \cdot \sqrt{7} = 2\sqrt{7}$

Dividing and Simplifying Radicals (p. 43)
1. $\sqrt{8} = \sqrt{4} \cdot \sqrt{2} = 2 \cdot \sqrt{2} = 2\sqrt{2}$
2. $\sqrt{12} = \sqrt{4} \cdot \sqrt{3} = 2 \cdot \sqrt{3} = 2\sqrt{3}$
3. $\sqrt{32} = \sqrt{4} \cdot \sqrt{8} = 2 \cdot \sqrt{8} = 2\sqrt{8}$ or
   $\sqrt{16} \cdot \sqrt{2} = 4 \cdot \sqrt{2} = 4\sqrt{2}$
4. $\sqrt{28} = \sqrt{4} \cdot \sqrt{7} = 2 \cdot \sqrt{7} = 2\sqrt{7}$

Finding the Value of the Unknown—I (p. 45)
2. 10, 10, 0, 11, $x = 11$, Check: 11
3. 17, 17, 0, 11, $v = 11$, Check: 11
4. $t = 8$ 5. $w = 6$ 6. $b = 17$
7. $n = 29$ 8. $y = 13$ 9. $x = 24$
10. $y = 24$ 11. $z = 18$ 12. $x = 49$
13. $n + 12 = 26$

Finding the Value of the Unknown—II (p. 46)
1. 3, 3, 0, 21, $y = 21$, Check: 21
2. 5, 5, 0, 25, $x = 25$, Check: 25
3. $b = 19$ 4. $t = 12$ 5. $w = 14$
6. $v = 4$ 7. $y = 3$ 8. $x = 13$
9. $x = 9$ 10. $t = -4$ 11. $y = 18$

Reviewing Simple Equations (p. 47)
1. mathematical, two   2. $x + 4$, 9
3. subtract
4. a. Choose any letter   b. 38
   c. $n - 38$ d. 64¢
5. $n - 6 = 12$ or $12 + 6 = n$; $n = 18$

Solving Equations With Multiplication (p. 48)
1. $x = 2$, 2   2. 14, 14, $x = 2$, 2
3. 8, 8, $x = 3$, 3
4. 5   5. 3   6. 8   7. 2
8. 2   9. 4   10. 11   11. 12
12. 8   13. 4   14. 14   15. 10

Solving Equations With Division (p. 49–50)
1. 4, 4, $y = 24$, 24, 6
2. 2, 2, $x = 14$, 14, 7
3. 5, 5, $t = 30$, Check: 30, 6
4. 8, 8, $w = 32$, Check: 32, 4 = 4
5. 9, 9, $p = 72$, Check: 72, 8 = 8
6. 3, 3, $x = 36$, Check: 36, 12 = 12
7. 12, 12, $y = 144$, Check: 144, 12 = 12
8. 16, 16, $c = 64$; Check: 64, 4 = 4
9. 2, 2, $x = 64$, Check: 64, 32 = 32
10. 3, 3, $y = 21$, Check: 21, 7 = 7

Ratios (p. 51)
1. 3 to 7   2. 2 to 9   3. 5 to 6
4. 4 to 7   5. 8 to 11   6. 2:3
7. 2:10   8. 1:5   9. 12:17
10. 9:13   11. $\frac{5}{12}$, 5 to 12, 5:12
12. $\frac{7}{12}$, 7 to 12, 7:12   13. $\frac{10}{5}$, 10 to 5, 10:5
14. $\frac{6}{4}$, 6 to 4, 6:4   15. $\frac{9}{11}$, 9 to 11, 9:11

Proportions (p. 52)
2. 5:3::10:6; 5 • 6 as 3 • 10
3. 1:3::3:9; 1 • 9 as 3 • 3
4. 3:5::9:15; 3 • 15 as 5 • 9
5. 2:3::4:6; 2 • 6 as 3 • 4
6. 5:7::10:14; 5 • 14 as 7 • 10
7. 3:8::6:16; 3 • 16 as 8 • 6
8. 9:1::27:3; 9 • 3 as 1 • 27

Cross Product Exercises (p. 53)
2. $2 \cdot 6 = 12$, $12 = 3x$, $\frac{12}{3} = \frac{3x}{3}$, $x = 4$
   $3 \cdot x = 3x$
3. $1 \cdot 8 = 8$, $8 = 4x$, $\frac{8}{4} = \frac{4x}{4}$, $x = 2$
   $4 \cdot x = 4x$
4. $1 \cdot 9 = 9$, $9 = 3x$, $\frac{9}{3} = \frac{3x}{3}$, $x = 3$
   $3 \cdot x = 3x$
5. $5 \cdot 12 = 60$, $60 = 6x$, $\frac{60}{6} = \frac{6x}{6}$, $x = 10$
   $6 \cdot x = 6x$
6. $1 \cdot 27 = 27$, $27 = 9x$, $\frac{27}{9} = \frac{9x}{9}$, $x = 3$
   $9 \cdot x = 9x$

Finding the Mean (p. 54)
Step 2. 12, 14, 14, 16, 16, 18, 20, 40, 150
Step 3. $150 \div 8 = 18.75$
Step 4. Mean = 18.75

1. 17; 2.8   2. 49; 7   3. 121; 15.1
4. 359; 59.8   5. 261; 32.6   6. 1,073; 178.8

Finding the Mode (p. 55)
Step 1. 12, 14, 14, 16, 16, 16, 18, 20, 40
Step 2. Mode = 16

1. 8   2. 12   3. 77
4. 31   5. 200   6. 11

Finding the Median (p. 56)
Step 1. 20, 24, 27, 30, 35, 38, 40, 42, 45
Step 3. Median = 35

1. 7   2. 57   3. 32
4. 187   5. 6   6. 8.5
7. 18.5

Probability (p. 57)
1. 1; 2   2. 1; 5   3. 1, 4
4. 3, 10   5. 2, 50   6. 1, 100

Probability Exercises (p. 58)
1. 3   2. 1   3. b   4. c   5. b
6. a   7. d   8. b   9. d

Probability Prediction (p. 59)
1. d   2. a   3. a   4. d
5. b   6. d   7. b   8. c

Learning About the Rectangular Coordinate System (p. 60)
1. 2, *x*-axis, positive   2. -4, *x*-axis, negative
3. -2, *y*-axis, negative   4. 4, *y*-axis, positive

Learning About Coordinates (p. 62)
1. -2, 3	2. 2, -1	3. -2, -6	4. 5, 9
5. -6, 6	6. -7, 2	7. -7, -6	8. 5, -6
9. 7, -3	10. 2, -7	11. 3, -4	12. -8, -3
13. -5	14. 3	15. -1	16. -2
17. 9	18. -6	20. 5	21. -6
22. -3	23. -3	24. -9	

Plotting the Point (p. 63)

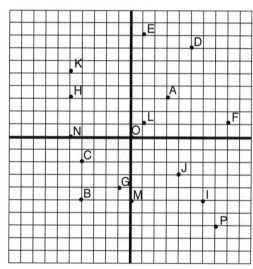

The Rectangular Coordinate System and Equations (p. 64)
Rectangular Coordinate System E

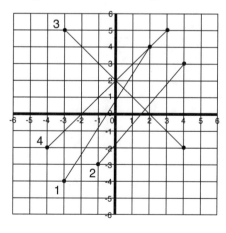

Rectangular Coordinate System F

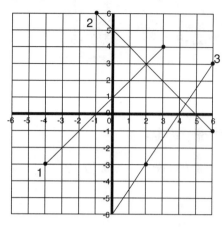

1. -1, 0; 0, 1   2. 5, 0; 0, 5   3. 4, 0; 0, -6

Linear Equations With Two Variables (p. 65)
1. 9, 8, 3   2. 6, 10, 4   3. 19, 17, 8
4. -20, -10, -5   5. 3, 4.5, 6   6. 1, 2, 8
7. 4, 16, -14   8. -7, -11, -15

Plotting Points for Linear Equations (p. 66–67)
1. 5, 3   2. 4, 2   3. 3, 1
4. -5, -7   5. 2, 0   6. -1, -3

Rectangular Coordinate System G

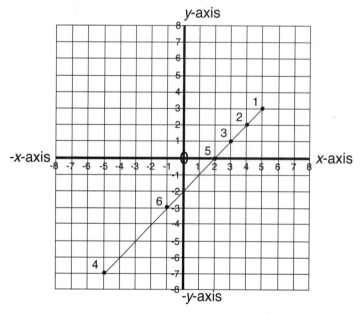

8. 2, 0   9. 0, -2   10. *x* = *y* + 2
11.–13. Plotted points will vary. Teacher check points and graph.

Finding the Slope and *y*-Intercept of a Straight Line (p. 69)

1. 2   2. -8   3. 0, -8

4. $y = 2x + 4$

5. $y = 2x + 1$

6. $y = \frac{1}{2}x - 3$ or $y = \frac{x}{2} - 3$

7. (0, 4)   8. (0, 1)   9. (0, -3)

Pre-Algebra is part of the Middle/Upper Grades Math Series, which provides students in middle school, junior high, and high school with instruction and practice in the fundamentals of math so they can transition to higher-order math concepts with confidence. Clear explanations, numerous practice exercises, and frequent reviews provide students with the tools for success in mastering pre-algebra.

Topics covered include:

- number systems

- integers

- variables & exponents

- roots & radicals

- factoring

- linear equations

- rectangular coordinate systems

Correlated to current national, state, and provincial standards

CD-405025

Mark Twain Media/Carson-Dellosa Publishing LLC

P.O. Box 35665
Greensboro NC 27425
www.carsondellosa.com

ISBN 1622237021 $11.99

51199

9 781622 237029